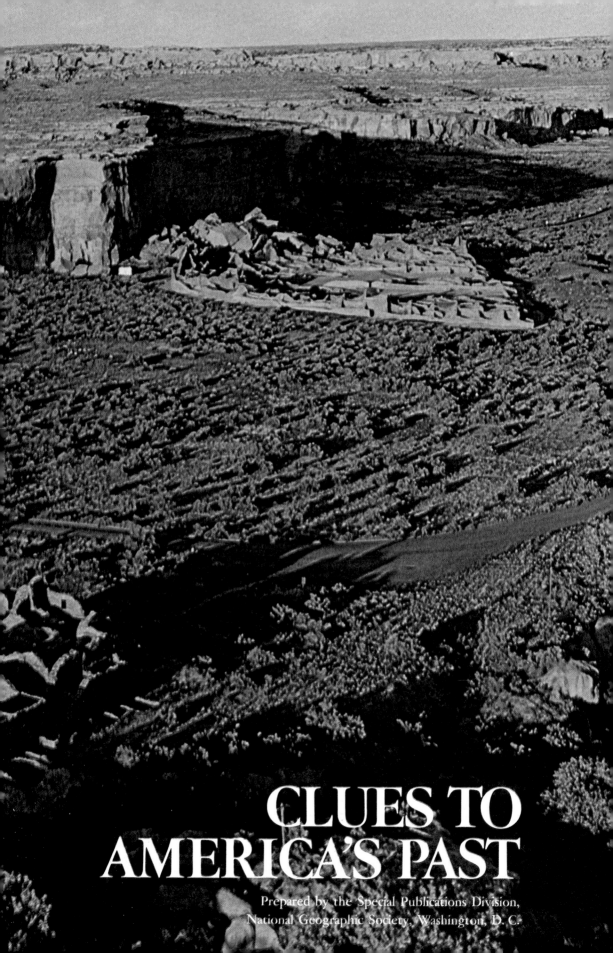

CLUES TO AMERICA'S PAST

Prepared by the Special Publications Division,
National Geographic Society, Washington, D. C.

CLUES TO AMERICA'S PAST

By Jeffrey P. Brain, Peter Copeland,
  Louis de la Haba, Mary Ann Harrell,
  Tee Loftin, Jay Luvaas,
  Douglas W. Schwartz
Paintings by Louis S. Glanzman

Published by
THE NATIONAL GEOGRAPHIC SOCIETY
ROBERT E. DOYLE, *President*
MELVILLE BELL GROSVENOR, *Editor-in-Chief*
GILBERT M. GROSVENOR, *Editor*

Prepared by
THE SPECIAL PUBLICATIONS DIVISION
ROBERT L. BREEDEN, *Editor*
DONALD J. CRUMP, *Associate Editor*
PHILIP B. SILCOTT, *Senior Editor*
MARY ANN HARRELL, *Managing Editor*
MARY G. BURNS, MARJORIE W. CLINE, PATRICIA
  F. FRAKES, BARBARA GRAZZINI, *Research*

Illustrations and Design
DAVID R. BRIDGE, *Picture Editor*
JOSEPHINE B. BOLT, *Art Director*
SUEZ KEHL, *Design Assistant*
MARIE A. BRADBY, LOUIS DE LA HABA,
  MARGARET MCKELWAY JOHNSON,
  TEE LOFTIN, LOUISA MAGZANIAN,
  JENNIFER C. URQUHART, *Picture Legends*
JOHN D. GARST, JR., MARGARET A. DEANE,
  MILDA R. STONE, TIBOR TOTH, *Maps*

Production and Printing
ROBERT W. MESSER, *Production Manager*
GEORGE V. WHITE, *Assistant Production Manager*
RAJA D. MURSHED, JUNE L. GRAHAM,
  CHRISTINE A. ROBERTS, *Production Assistants*
JOHN R. METCALFE, *Engraving and Printing*
JANE H. BUXTON, STEPHANIE S. COOKE,
  MARY C. HUMPHREYS, SUZANNE J. JACOBSON,
  CLEO PETROFF, MARILYN L. WILBUR,
  LINDA M. YEE, *Staff Assistants*
GEORGE I. BURNESTON, III, *Index*

*Overleaf: Thousand-year-old ruins cast long shadows
in northwest New Mexico's Chaco Canyon. Page 1:
A masked figure apparently enacts a ritual now
unknown—a painting on a Mimbres bowl some 900
years old, from New Mexico. Endpapers: Mimbres
bowls reveal the potters' distinctive portrayals of
living beings as well as the geometric designs typical
of the Southwest. Bookbinding: An eagle in embossed
sheet copper, from an Indian mound in Illinois,
represents the continuities of America's long past.*

OVERLEAF: DAVID HISER. PAGE 1: HILLEL BURGER, PEABODY
MUSEUM OF ARCHAEOLOGY AND ETHNOLOGY. ENDPAPERS:
N.G.S. PHOTOGRAPHER JOSEPH H. BAILEY. BOOKBINDING:
SMITHSONIAN INSTITUTION; COTTON COULSON

COTTON COULSON

*Pilgrim for a day, dance director Laurie
Downing claps the beat as she leads merry-
makers in a 17th-century country dance—
part of a festival re-enactment at Plimoth
Plantation in Massachusetts. Historical
research has shown the Pilgrims' harvest
feast in 1621 as one of games and sports,
not the solemn "thanksgiving" of tradition.*

Foreword

As an archeologist, I often find myself speculating on what will be available to my counterparts of the future to interpret the world we live in today.

Take my living room, for example. Barring a protective shower of volcanic ash or a sudden mudslide — unlikely, I hope, in Chapel Hill, North Carolina — neither my wooden house nor most of its contents will survive even a thousand years. Moisture and insects would make short work of cloth, books, and papers. Perhaps some metal or glass would endure in recognizable form — say, parts of the stereo system, or doorknobs, or andirons.

The clay flowerpots would last even if they broke; but since many of mine were made by Mexican potters, perhaps they would only cause confusion. If they didn't, doubtless my cast of an eighth-century Maya bas-relief would.

In fact, whether or not *anything* in my house (or yours) would be recognizable depends on how much the future excavator would know about late 20th-century crafts and technology and their cultural context. Some of our artifacts are highly specialized. How readily can you identify a *crêpes* griddle, or a spring winder, or a light-bulb grabber? A spark-plug gapper? A swivel-grip oil-filter wrench?

To go a step further, in the future: How would the inventory of artifacts and their distribution at my house compare with those from other houses on my block? Or with inventories from house mounds on the suburban fringes of Seattle?

Such mental games are more than diversion. They help keep me aware of the problems archeologists confront in trying to know *what* took place during man's millions of yesterdays, *when* it took place, and — best of all — *why.*

This book is about clues to our own past, a tremendous span of time that has increased slightly even as you read these words. But the clues are just the beginning in stories of luck, of demanding labor, and of logic. For only by meticulous scholarship can we bridge the gap between the tangible world of surviving tools, ornaments, and buildings, and the invisible world of human behavior — the ways people worshiped, played, and organized their lives in societies.

In the chapters that follow, you will see many vignettes of America's yesterdays, from a Paleo-Indian hunting ceremony of some 10,000 years ago to the nostalgic times of living memory when anything from comic books to last week's torn-down landmark is fair game. You will see how willow-branch figurines reveal an unknown chapter in the life of early man in the Grand Canyon; how an archeologist working in Nevada "predicts the past"; even how a sacked shipwreck reflects timber shortages in 17th-century Europe. And how documents, both the truthful and the deceptive ones, let us enter that invisible world of history.

However sparse some of its evidence may be, the past is truly all around us. The methods of knowing it are many. It is heartening to see how those who deal with it — as scholars and as citizens alert to its value — help us recapitulate our complex heritage.

GEORGE E. STUART
Archeologist, National Geographic Society

Contents

Archeologist Peter Eschman uses a dental pick to clean soil deposits grain by grain from a 10,000-year-old bison jaw — evidence of a successful hunt — at the Jones-Miller Paleo-Indian site near Wray, Colorado.

NEW LANDS, NEW LIVES:

THE LAST FEW MINUTES of picking our way up the rocks brought us to the opening in the great Redwall formation. From here I could look both into the cave mouth and over the magnificent Grand Canyon. I called to my companion Art Lange, "We've been climbing for nearly an hour—let's stop for a breather before we go in."

My pack was getting heavier than I cared to say, and I sank down on the nearest rock. A slight dizziness from the climb came over me, and my mind began drifting back to the beginning of all this.

One summer night the year before, I was sitting by a campfire on the South Rim when Art and Raymond deSaussure came up and introduced themselves. They explained that they had been conducting a survey of caves: "So far Ray and I have been in 150 caves in the Canyon. In four, something very curious has shown up that perhaps you can explain to us."

They described small fragments of twisted and tied willow branches, obviously man-made, and one little figurine of this material. It sounded like nothing I was familiar with, and I was not prepared for the object they showed me.

It was by far the most appealing artifact I had ever seen, not quite the size of my hand, in the form of a deerlike animal with a definite ageless charm.

Since I hoped to learn as much as possible about the total prehistory of the Canyon, I didn't hesitate to say, "Let's put together a small expedition and see what we can learn about this."

A year later the arrangements were made, with a small sum of money raised for food and supplies. On a bright moonlit August night, each with a 60-pound pack, we descended the Kaibab trail. By midmorning we had reached a side canyon called "Cremation" and the sun was beaming down. "I know exactly how this place was named," Ray remarked. Soon, more slowly now, we were climbing the talus slope to our destination.

"What's your plan when we start in there?" Art's voice brought me back to the present and I turned to stare at the cave. Beyond an entrance littered with huge boulders, a dusty, fairly flat floor reached back into darkness.

Authoritatively, I said, "We should excavate some test pits with precise stratigraphic levels in the cave floor near the entrance. That's where the people probably lived and where most of their trash should be. From these remains we can reconstruct the whole story and fit the figurines into their way of life." All this was announced with the complete confidence possessed only by a new Ph.D.

I had just completed my doctoral dissertation on the prehistory of a side canyon. In 1955 almost no archeological work had been carried out in the Grand Canyon itself. It appeared that Indian farmers had settled the rim areas in the eighth century of the Christian era and gradually worked their way into the canyon proper; but all this was still a rather hazy outline. I had no idea that this cave expedition would provide a new dimension for the story.

Next morning we began digging. In semidarkness, we measured our precise three-meter squares and ten-centimeter

A NEW WORLD REVEALED

levels so we could plot the location of everything we found. Carefully I examined each shovelful, knowing the answers must lie just below. Once we reached an indication of cultural materials, we would use trowels and camel's hair brushes. After three days I finally admitted to myself that I was completely wrong. Absolutely nothing had shown up.

To cover my embarrassment, I said, "Well, at least we know *for sure* they didn't live in this cave. The question now is, did you two find the only figurine? And if so, how did it get here?"

As we disconsolately packed to leave, I wandered around the edges of the cave, flashlight in hand. I had barely seen these areas because of the tunnel vision created by my certainty of how to proceed. Now, in a pack rat's nest, I spotted fragments of twisted willow — and then my eyes focused on a pile of rock two feet high. It looked suspiciously unnatural, like a cairn piled on a mountaintop by climbers.

I shouted for Art and Ray.

They came rushing over, and we examined the area quickly.

With enthusiastic caution, we peeled back the rocks and at the bottom of the pile we saw twisted willow through the dust. We photographed and recorded each item, then dusted it off *in situ* — in place — with a paintbrush. When we finished, we counted 32 complete figurines in one small scooped-out basin.

Gradually we removed each one. As we did, we noted its depth, orientation, and

(Continued on page 16)

An Overview
of Discovery and
Development
in American
Archeology

By DOUGLAS W. SCHWARTZ
Director, School of American Research

FIST-SIZE POT, CONTAINING CORN POLLEN, FOUND BENEATH
A KIVA FLOOR IN EXCAVATIONS AT ARROYO HONDO, NEW MEXICO.

Willow-twig effigies from a Grand Canyon cave probably represent mountain sheep, says author Douglas W. Schwartz. He discovered them in 1955. Dozens

like them have turned up in remote caves above side canyons leading to the Colorado River. Placed there by unknown Indians some 4,000 years ago, the effigies almost certainly figured in rituals conducted to ensure success in the hunt — some had been pierced with miniature spears. Above, a hunter's view from inside one of the figurine caves; opposite, the desolate landscape the hunting parties would have traveled, below the Canyon's North Rim.

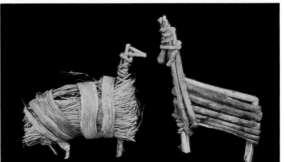

DAVID GRANT NOBLE (ABOVE AND BELOW)

SCHOOL OF AMERICAN RESEARCH (ABOVE)

With shovels in reserve, an archeology crew attacks a sterile overburden of wind-blown sand that covered a pueblo at Arroyo Hondo, New Mexico. At center left, the author, who directed the excavation, discusses its progress with two crew chiefs—Michael Marshall, left, and Richard Lang. "They're good dirt archeologists—that's why they're talking and I'm listening," he says. A hot-air balloon hovers over the partially cleared site, providing a stable platform for photography and mapping. Twice occupied and twice deserted between A.D. 1285 and 1425, Arroyo Hondo housed an Indian farming community of a thousand people at its peak. Tree-ring and pollen analyses indicate that lack of rainfall drove residents from the Sangre de Cristo foothills, presumably to sites on the floodplains of the Rio Grande.

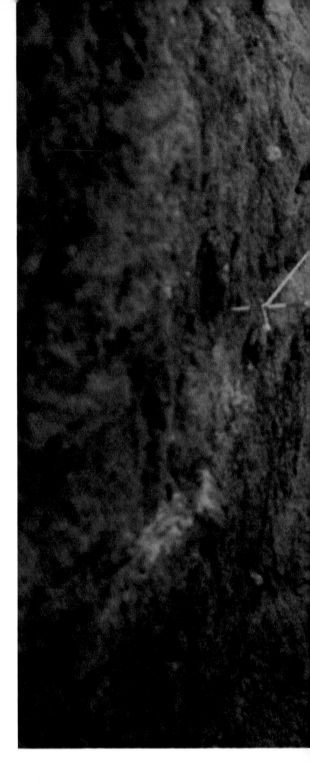

*Swept-up dust engulfs workers clearing a kiva —
a ceremonial chamber—at Arroyo Hondo. Test
trenches like that in the foreground revealed its
presence. At upper left, a collared lizard clings*

to an ancient adobe wall. At left, in its 14th-century grave, an adult skull.
Such burials sometimes contain leather blankets or yucca mats, but not so often as
those of the young. Arroyo Hondo's people had few grave goods and no formal
cemetery; they interred their dead in plazas, under rooms, or even in trash heaps.

its placement in relationship to the others, for at this point we had no idea what might be important and we certainly did not want to miss anything. We noted that shredded juniper bark and clumps of grass had been placed between layers of figurines.

Each figurine was about the size of a small hand and made of a single twig of willow. Some had what appeared to be horns and some a wrapping of grass around the body, but all were obviously made to a pattern.

As I pondered their function, several clues were obvious. The figurines were found in caves not used for living purposes and not easy of access. Their presence under the rock cairn suggested a special importance. Moreover, several had been pierced with small sticks — undoubtedly, miniature spears.

Down the centuries and throughout the world, people have believed that they can control supernatural powers by following magical rituals. One method anthropologists have called imitative magic, and Sir James Frazer in his great work *The Golden Bough* described a classic example: "when...an Ojebway Indian desires to work evil on any one, he makes a little wooden image of his enemy and runs a needle into its head or heart, or shoots an arrow into it, believing that wherever the needle pierces or the arrow strikes the image, his foe will at the same instant be seized with a sharp pain...."

We all know this process from voodoo rites in those B movies we saw as kids — and all its elements were apparent in the figurine caves of the Grand Canyon.

Further clues led us to identify the effigies as of mountain sheep, and a picture of the past began to emerge. A few men hiked into the Canyon, collected willow branches from trees near a spring, and headed up a side canyon to a cave visited only on special occasions. Then, following an age-old ritual, they carefully split the twigs and fashioned the figurines. They scooped out a basin in the cave floor and "speared" some of the figurines. They were simulating actions to be carried out in the hours ahead — probably near a spring, where mountain sheep can be stalked by clever hunters. What incantations they performed we will never know, but when all was completed the hunters left secure in the knowledge that they had done everything possible to ensure success.

The exhilaration that followed this breakthrough was one I will never forget. There is something almost mystical in realizing you have indeed stepped back in time and seen in some detail the life of another people. And therein lies the reward and frustration of archeology: to visit the past, only to be trapped by a fog that just occasionally allows a partial and tantalizing view.

I submitted figurine fragments to a laboratory for radiocarbon dating, a method just coming into wide use. I was suspicious of the results, but a second lab confirmed them. The figurines had been made more than 4,000 years ago!

From work done elsewhere — by Ted Sayles and Paul Martin in Arizona and Jesse Jennings in Utah — I knew that life for the figurine-makers would have re-

volved around hunting and gathering. It would be hundreds of years before their descendants would acquire the ideas and materials needed for growing crops. Their life would have been a constant round of collecting wild plants and hunting or trapping wild animals, all within a rather large and varied territory.

Reconstructing such a life requires knowledge of the particular environment and of lives led by other peoples at the same level of culture — in this case, people like the Paiute of the Great Basin, the Bushmen of South Africa, or the Australian Aborigines.

Such evidence suggests that each year bands of three or four extended families, some 25 or 30 persons in all, would roam in a definite pattern, seeking the best resources of the season.

In spring and summer, women must have collected buds and fruits and seeds in the varied environments of the canyon and the plateau. Men would have hunted migratory waterfowl in season. In autumn, in years when piñon nuts were especially abundant, all would have joined in collecting this highly nutritious food in the South

Surrounded by rooms, a plaza at Arroyo Hondo served as a social, ceremonial, and work center. Here pueblo dwellers made stone tools, prepared food, and conducted rituals in the two kivas. Below, staples of the local diet.

*Increasing complexity of design and decoration
—clues in themselves to chronology and cultural
links—characterizes a series of pots from the
Southwest. From bottom: a smoke-stained utility*

Rim forests. And in the cold winters men certainly stalked mountain sheep at water holes or springs of the side canyons, faithfully enacting the ritual of the figurines.

Shelters would be of simple construction, perhaps just windbreaks of brush. Little trash would accumulate and less would survive—items like pine boughs for sleeping nests. Valuables like rabbit-fur blankets and stone knives would be left only if damaged beyond repair. It was long before the time of pottery, which first appeared on the Canyon rim about A.D. 600.

During one of our long, hot inner-canyon evenings, Ray summed up the matter: "How ironic. We seem to have discovered so much about one small part of what must have been secret ritual, while much of their everyday life will probably always remain at the level of mere speculation." Regretfully, I agreed.

Almost a quarter of a century has passed. More figurines have been found in the caves of the region. Much has been learned about its ecology. But Ray's prediction has held true.

Yet I have always felt fortunate that this was my first professional project, since it contained so many of the elements that make the study of the past such a fascinating field. The adventure and excitement of the unknown. The systematic work leading to the accumulation of small clues. The conclusions drawn, some based on the immediate data and some from secondary inferences. And then the reconstruction of part of the past.

Looking back, I'm not sorry that I was dealing with a hunting band while some of my friends were beginning work on temple mounds in the Mississippi Valley or great Maya cities. Later I was to direct complex projects that took years to excavate and a decade to unravel, but here in one season I could see a project through and gain a rare insight into a way of life similar to that of our own remote ancestors and those of the American Indian.

Interest and excitement about the past have deep roots in America. Almost as soon as European settlers reached these shores, there was speculation about the stone tools and carvings found in woods or turned up by plows. Earthworks, especially, suggested a notable prehistory.

Yet such remains were not considered old at all by present standards, certainly no more than a thousand years. This, of course, reflected the age of the earth proposed by Biblical scholars. Further, a single culture was thought responsible for all prehistoric materials and this was variously identified—one of the Lost Tribes of Israel, the Welsh, ancient Egyptians or Phoenicians, or occupants of the lost continents of Atlantis or Mu. Whoever they were, many Americans assumed, they could not have been ancestors of those ferocious, impoverished Indians seen over the sights of a gun.

An early exception to this uncritical speculation was one of the geniuses of this country—Thomas Jefferson. While many thought of Indians simply as enemies and inferiors, he saw them differently. In a letter dated 1808, President Jefferson wrote to the Mohicans and other eastern tribes: "you will mix with us by marriage, your blood will run in our veins, and will spread with us over this great island."

*jar from Arroyo Hondo; a 12th-century Sosi black-on-white bowl from the
Grand Canyon; a Mimbres painted bowl from New Mexico, a style unique
in its portrayal of living creatures; a 14th-century bowl from Arroyo Hondo;
a constricted-mouth jar from Santo Domingo Pueblo in the Rio Grande valley.*

The leading European naturalist, Count Georges de Buffon, had argued that a "degenerative" process had operated in North America, making its inhabitants smaller and weaker in intelligence than Europeans. Jefferson attacked this notion, saying the Indian in "vivacity and activity of mind was fully equal to a white man."

While others were merely discussing the prehistoric remains found in the East, Jefferson approached the issue as an intuitive scientist. In his *Notes on the State of Virginia,* written in 1781, he discussed the earthen mounds "found all over this country." These were known to hold bones of the dead, but there was uncertainty about their use: for the burial of slain warriors on a battleground, for a single interment of individuals who had died over a period of time, for the "sepulchers" of a particular town? He wrote in his journal: "There being one of these in my neighbourhood, I wished to satisfy myself whether any, and which of these opinions were just."

First he probed the mound "superficially" and determined the depths at which he came upon human bone — six inches to three feet. Confident that he knew the general nature of the mound, he made "a perpendicular cut through . . . the barrow, that I might examine its internal structure." At the bottom he found stratified layers of bones, interlain with rock and earth: four strata at one end, three at the other. He "conjectured" that the mound contained a thousand skeletons. Finding no sign of wounds, but some bones of infants and children, he ruled out the theory of "war dead." From evidence of differential

*With its back to a cliff,
Pueblo Bonito faces New
Mexico's Chaco River. At
this D-shaped pueblo
early southwestern
agriculturalists lived in
apartments that rose four
stories high in places;
they worshiped in circular
underground kivas.
Pueblo Bonito's first
settlers arrived about
A.D. 900. Climatic
change—or inter-pueblo
dissension—may have
caused its abandonment
about 300 years later.
The author has called
Pueblo Bonito "one of
the most beautiful
archeological structures
in the world." The name
itself supports his view;*
bonito *in Spanish
means "beautiful."*

From Chaco Canyon's sandstone, Indian
architects shaped building blocks. Styles of
veneer for the rubble-filled walls appear at
left: Old Bonitian, Three, Late Bonitian.
Dr. Neil M. Judd, the pueblo's excavator,
recorded his considered praise for earlier,
"cruder" stonework as well as its successors.
"Late Bonitian masonry," he wrote,
"has won . . . a reputation . . . for all time."

decay, he deduced burials over some span of time; from the "confused" disorder of the bones, he deduced the "accustomary collection" for a final burial.

Truly his method foreshadowed that of recent work: the carefully framed question, the systematic collection of evidence, the careful consideration of it, and the reasoned conclusion.

More than half a century passed before others began to live up to his sagacity; but by the 1850's a new approach began to emerge, emphasizing the procedures so natural to Jefferson.

Now a more complex picture of America's past began to emerge, with a realization that Indians, not some "lost race," had created these prehistoric remains. The past lengthened, as the timetables of geology gained wider acceptance. Step by step, the beginnings and content of prehistory were pushed backward. After World War II, when atomic-bomb research gave us radiocarbon dating as a byproduct, the longest steps were taken.

Today we feel confident in saying that man must have reached this continent more than 25,000 years ago. This book reports current work at sites like the Meadowcroft rock shelter in western Pennsylvania, where occupation for some 16 millennia has now been documented. With such corroboration, these once-unthinkably early dates seem relatively safe.

Within this century, an increase in systematic work over the continent has revealed the complexity of early cultures. It has also confirmed another shrewd hypothesis of Jefferson's, the Asiatic origin of the American Indian.

The alternatives die hard, and feature writers still make colorful copy of proposed Phoenician or Egyptian links with the Indians. There are indeed indications that other peoples have made occasional landfalls in the Western Hemisphere, accidentally or not. In addition to the Vikings, mariners from Japan and Polynesia may have reached the Americas.

Nevertheless, our best evidence supports the view that a land bridge between Siberia and Alaska was the route of entry for the ancestors of the American Indian. During the Ice Age, water accumulated in huge glaciers and continental ice sheets until worldwide ocean levels dropped by as much as 400 feet. The shallows of Bering Strait became open tundra. Across this land, possibly a thousand miles wide, the earliest people made their way.

Why did they come? Not as self-conscious migrants, certainly. They lived as hunting and gathering bands. It is easy to see how the younger hunters would have to find other ranges when the people grew too numerous for food resources on home ground. As population pressures increased, a band would create a new territory for its members — and so they entered this new land that had never before been hunted by men.

They made their way southward, and eastward, beyond the margins of the ice sheets, taking perhaps 20,000 years to traverse the land masses of the hemisphere. By 8000 B.C. we find evidence of the presence of their descendants at the southern tip of South America. If the outlines of the story are clear, the details remain to be filled in.

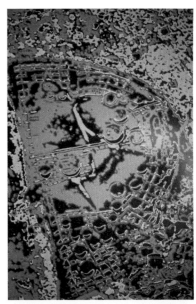

The Ice Age petered out to its unspectacular end. Its distinctive fauna disappeared, the big game of the Pleistocene: the giant ground sloth, the mammoth, the oversize bison. Their extinction is a matter of controversy, but some of us believe they were hunted out of existence by the early or Paleo-Indians; and with them vanished the great predators — sabertooth cats and dire wolves.

In the so-called Archaic times that followed, new ways of life began to develop, basically resembling the type reflected in the figurine caves but differing in response to local environments.

Then, before the beginning of the Christian era, corn and other crops — developed in Mexico — began to appear farther north. Gradually the hunting and gathering life began to include the cultivation of food in suitable areas. By the beginning of the historic period, more than a dozen major cultural configurations were present and each had its own intricate development.

I've recently discussed one of these with Stuart Streuver of Northwestern University, who calls a 3,000-square-mile

Remote-sensing technology simplifies images for archeologists. For one black-and-white photograph of Pueblo Bonito, they assign selected colors to shades of gray on the film, with an instrument named a Digicol Color Monitor. Above, yellow or orange brings out roads and walls; blue, bare soil. By a technique called edge enhancement, the Digicol system could make visible miles of prehistoric roads in the high-altitude view above.

Decorated sherds record the Hopewell culture, notable in the prehistoric Midwest. Kenneth B. Farnsworth sorts ware from the Loy site in Illinois; Nora Groce assembles the rim of a 1,900-year-old cauldron that still held charred food. With it excavators found two-inch deposits of fish bones—apparently cooks kept stew at a perpetual simmer, without set times for meals. Archeologist Philip Phillips wryly calls such drab sherds "hopelessly unendearing," but they have immense value for understanding the past.

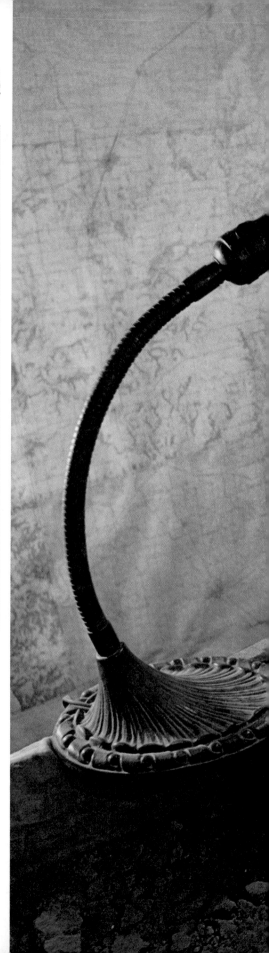

area of the Illinois River Valley his "research universe."

"After seven years of work," he said, "we understood all there was to know about its prehistoric settlements. But in 1968 we found a new kind of site — outside the known range." This is the Koster site, near Kampsville, Illinois. Here Stu and his crew of 70 have screened the equivalent of 560 dump-truck loads of soil to explore a settlement site used almost continuously for perhaps 9,000 years.

"It began about 15 minutes after the end of the Ice Age," Stu said in his colorful style, "and went on with few if any major interruptions until 1200 A.D."

Steep slopes shelter the site on three sides, he explained. If people denuded the hillsides for firewood and housebuilding, erosion would make the site unusable until new trees matured. Thus deposits of sterile soil separate some 14 horizons, or layers, of village remains. Surprisingly, the early villages sustained a settled life without planting crops.

I asked Stu if he could make any generalizations about this vast period of time, and he launched enthusiastically into describing a stable pattern: "I see no significant change in the way of life from soon after the initial occupation until about 200 B.C. — when we date the beginnings of the Hopewell culture.

"That's 300 or more generations without cataclysmic starvation, population explosion, or warfare. If I'm reading the archeological record correctly, that's pretty good for people whose energy control was minuscule compared to ours."

Stu's voice grew reflective as we dis-cussed factors that might have kept this population stable. My own work involves the mystery of prehistoric population structure and dynamics. I've found extreme fluctuations in just over a century while he had found stability over thousands of years. Both of us are probing for explanations, weighing possibilities that cannot yet be called answers.

Three other major sites will suggest the range of prehistoric adaptations and artistic creativity, as well as the range of archeological approaches necessary for their recovery. My Arctic example is vivid in my mind after a recent tour by bush plane over proposed national parks to be established in Alaska.

We were flying north over the sea, just crossing the Arctic Circle, when the co-pilot shouted, "Look down! Just off the left wing! Beluga whales!" We were low over the blue water and I nearly jumped from my seat at the view: more than twenty whales sunning near the surface, occasionally rising to reveal white skin. The Arctic was truly surrounding us: snow mountains rising ahead, ice floes drifting below, and these great animals swimming gracefully among them. I could easily visualize Eskimos in kayaks paddling up for the hunt and feel the cold biting into their faces.

No people ever fought such a heroic battle for survival, every day of their lives. Yet their prehistory is one of sustained success against great odds, and constant improvement in their complex technology for use in a harsh environment.

North of Kotzebue Sound, its shores still ice-bound in June, our destination

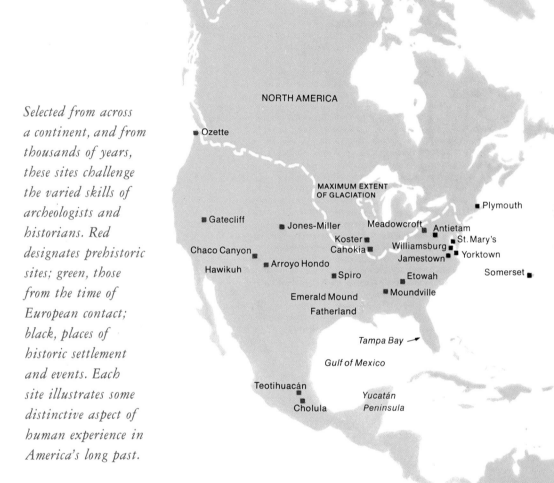

Selected from across a continent, and from thousands of years, these sites challenge the varied skills of archeologists and historians. Red designates prehistoric sites; green, those from the time of European contact; black, places of historic settlement and events. Each site illustrates some distinctive aspect of human experience in America's long past.

Bering Strait ∎ Ipiutak

NORTH AMERICA

∎ Ozette

MAXIMUM EXTENT
OF GLACIATION

∎ Plymouth

∎ Gatecliff   ∎ Jones-Miller   Meadowcroft ∎   ∎ Antietam

Koster ∎   Williamsburg ∎ ∎ St. Mary's

Chaco Canyon ∎   Cahokia ∎   Jamestown ∎ ∎ Yorktown

Hawikuh ∎   ∎ Arroyo Hondo   Etowah ∎   Somerset ∎

∎ Spiro   ∎ Moundville

Emerald Mound ∎
Fatherland

Tampa Bay →

Gulf of Mexico

Teotihuacán ∎   Yucatán
Peninsula
Cholula ∎

SOUTH AMERICA

came into view: Cape Krusenstern. A colleague spotted it first. "It looks like a bunch of crescent moons stacked next to each other," he yelled. Since the great glacial ice of the Pleistocene began melting away, this land has been rising, exposing a vast expanse of beaches. For centuries men have used these beaches for fishing and hunting. At intervals over the years, as the strand rose and widened, the Eskimos would move their camps closer to the water and leave varied remains behind. Scores of times this happened.

In Alaska's frigid wastes, hunters of a village called Ipiutak pull a walrus onto an ice floe. At their settlement on Point Hope, as many as 4,000 people lived between A.D. 1 and 500, hunting walrus and seal from early spring through summer, moving inland in winter to stalk

caribou. From walrus ivory the Ipiutak craftsmen carved harpoon points, which they armed with sharp flint blades. From walrus rawhide they made line. Archeologist Froelich Rainey, who dug the site, describes this as "the strongest line known before the invention of the steel cable."

Today, while camps are still built on the latest beach, the cape is a time-ordered encyclopedia of Eskimo prehistory, waiting for the archeologist to continue reading its pages.

"Can we fly just a hundred miles farther?" I pleaded with the pilot, for northward, at Point Hope, lies one of the great sites of Arctic archeology, Ipiutak. He refused, for lack of fuel, but I had to make the effort at least.

At Ipiutak from 1939 to 1941 Helge Larsen and Froelich Rainey had excavated a village about 1,500 or 1,800 years old. They estimated that within about a century some 800 log-and-sod houses were built here. Spring brought the ancient hunters to the coast for seal and walrus; winter took them inland for caribou.

Complex toggle harpoon gear would mark this culture as Eskimo. Ipiutak is unique, however, because of its flamboyant ivory carvings. Its shallow graves yielded small sculptures of walruses, bears, and other natural as well as fantastic animals. Even everyday utensils were adorned with animal heads: harpoon sockets, dagger hilts, knife handles. The excavations also revealed fine, enigmatic objects carved in spirals, and linked chains of ivory.

"Ipiutak's still a puzzle after thirty years of digging in the Arctic," Froe Rainey commented recently. "It's more of an enigma than ever. There's nothing quite like it. For one thing, it's such an unusually large settlement—why was it here? And it has a complex of items that don't show up anywhere else, including delicate flint blades, and small engraving tools that must have been tipped with iron or steel.

"Many of the carvings resemble metal ornaments worn by shamans in Siberia— the famous 'Siberian animal style' that's seen in Scythian designs. I suspect all this reflects trade with Asia, perhaps as far as the Ural Mountains in Russia. You know, walrus rawhide made the strongest line known before steel cable, and walrus ivory was thought to have mystical qualities. Ipiutak's a good place for walrus hunting, one of the best. But I don't have any real proof of a trade network—just these clues." Whatever Ipiutak's carvings meant to their makers, we agreed, they represent outstanding achievement in one of the distinctive art styles of prehistoric America.

As I flew home from the Alaska trip, the great forests of the Northwest lay below me cloaked in fog. In that mist, I knew, my old friend Dick Daugherty from Washington State University would be working at a most interesting site called Ozette. On the Pacific coast south of the entrance to Juan de Fuca Strait, Dick and his co-workers have been excavating a series of houses 300 to 500 years old.

Ozette is a sort of New World Pompeii. Mudslides from a hill covered the waterside homes and preserved many rare items made from wood or plant fibers.

"The mudslides carried away parts of walls, but it's surprising how many things survived undamaged," Dick told me one evening at my home in Santa Fe.

"You know, these homes were inhabited by ancestors of the Makah tribe, and I'm really excited about the fact that the Makah have been an important part of the

resembles Shang burial masks from China. A profusion of grave goods indicates a ghost cult among the Ipiutak people.

whole project. They fixed up a lab for us. They have students working there and in the University of Washington's museum training program—they're planning to develop and staff their own museum on their site."

Archeologists like to swap the latest news, and Dick and I talked late into the night about the wonders of Ozette. By a crackling fire, he told me how winter storms interrupt operations at the site for as long as a week at a time. The 40 to 50 students who work in summer "almost get used to the cool climate with lots of rain, emphasis on *lots.*" He gazed into the fire, pulled on his pipe, and said, "I guess on our site, happiness is being warm and dry at the same time."

Dick showed me photographs of the splendid range of finds: carved bowls, embossed effigies, ornate war clubs, seal-killer clubs. "Some anthropologists have argued that this kind of woodworking developed only after European contact, with metal tools, but the work at Ozette establishes a developed skill and art style at least a century earlier!"

I did get a word in edgewise about my own most recent work at Arroyo Hondo, a thousand-room pueblo site in northern New Mexico. In the high, mountain-bordered Rio Grande valley, we work through the summer. (We have low humidity but frequent gusty winds, and happiness is rinsing away dust and cooling off.) Here for four field seasons we explored the culture of Indian farmers in the 14th century.

We could date the site with the precision that archeologists enjoy in the

Openwork carvings in ivory, such as the one below, distinguish Ipiutak from Eskimo sites. This piece looks like a swivel used in dog harnesses, but Siberian shamans wore such objects on their parkas. Other ivory carvings echo the style of Siberian ritual items in iron and bronze. Dr. Rainey speculates that Ipiutak had cultural links with metal-using peoples of Russia because of trade, exporting both its rawhide and its ivory, thought in Asia to have magical virtues.

"Pompeii in mud ... an archeologist's dream."
Thus Dr. Richard D. Daugherty (below)
describes the excavation at Ozette, in northwest
Washington State. Some three centuries ago,
mudslides buried houses of a Makah Indian
community, preserving the contents as if time
had stopped. So far, Dr. Daugherty's team has
found more than 45,000 artifacts, including
this heavy owl-headed club and the fragile
antler or sea-lion-tooth statuette below it.
Dr. Daugherty shows a seal-killer club to a
group of Makah women, whose tribal council
has written: "We Makahs look in a special way
at what is coming from the mud at Ozette, for
this is our heritage." A Makah archeology
student, Mari Flinn, works at the site; others
will build and staff a Makah-sponsored
museum to house the treasures of Ozette.

Southwest, thanks to tree rings from timbers used by the builders. Construction began about A.D. 1285, with extensions and repairs continuing to its final abandonment in 1425.

We noted a change in floor plans, from the early five-room ground-floor "apartments" to later units of two rooms. This may well reflect a change in family life and social organization.

But our work involved a great deal more than just digging rooms and plazas. Palynologists studied pollen from the floors to help determine the nature of the prehistoric environment. Ecologists tested soils looking for the most probable location of prehistoric fields, and grew sample crops. Paleobotanists analyzed remains of wild and cultivated plants to help reconstruct the diet of the ancient inhabitants, while zoologists identified the bones of domestic turkeys and of animals hunted in the forests and grasslands nearby.

Thus we collected evidence for the use of natural resources in good years, and therefore we could interpret what happened in this marginal environment in years of lessening rainfall. Food supplies failed. The bones of children reveal signs of malnutrition.

We could almost hear older people deciding to stay and tough it out: "This is my home. I was born here. I know this land. I have always worked here. My spirits are here." And young couples deciding to leave: "We must have more food for the children. We must join our kin on the good land down by the Great River."

In all of this, we had a traditional archeological purpose of trying to reconstruct a specific culture. But I was equally interested in another objective, of cross-cultural study. With our traditional purpose achieved, we knew that the population of Arroyo Hondo had increased from three families to more than a thousand people in just over one generation—the kind of increase we see in our cities and suburbs today.

Now I want to use Arroyo Hondo as a laboratory, to study the relationship between rapid population growth and cultural change. Such events have challenged many peoples, repeatedly, over the centuries; today they have a special urgency. We hope to deal with a universal problem, using the resources of the past.

This kind of complex, multidisciplinary, large-scale project—at Koster or Ozette or Arroyo Hondo, or many other sites—offers an obvious contrast to my work nearly a quarter of a century ago in the figurine caves. (To say nothing of the collect-handsome-specimens procedures of earlier decades!) And these differences reflect the growth in techniques and objectives of archeology generally.

During these two eventful decades the discipline of archeology has been changing dramatically. Now relative chronology and pure description are just a beginning. We no longer see as our only task the identification and documentation of vanished lifeways. Our current work includes notable successes in this, as Lou de la Haba reports in this book, but it's part of a larger purpose.

We don't even confine our aims to explaining how such lifeways led to the remarkable cultures that Europeans found

in North America. This is an epic in its own right; and Jeff Brain tells how he and his colleagues are working out the story in the lower Mississippi Valley — confirming, incidentally, details once dismissed as sheer romance.

Now we can prove that prehistoric cultures changed through the years, and we want to explain why. Perhaps this will help us reach an understanding of cultural origin, alteration, and collapse wherever it occurs.

I don't want to oversell archeology. We're far from being able to state laws of cultural change. Some of us think we'll never be able to. Still, ours is a young science, and many of us believe devoutly that the past can help enlighten the future if not foretell its details.

Already, as this book shows, archeology can bring freshness and solidity not only to prehistory but also to the times of written record and national legend. Trade on the Spanish Main, a famous day for the Plymouth colonists, plantation life before the Revolution — we may think we know them well. But Peter Copeland and Tee Loftin have some new detective work to sharpen our appreciation of them; and Jay Luvaas shows what sturdy boots and spadework mean to understanding events as complicated as the siege at Yorktown and the decisive battle at Antietam.

So with our colleagues the historians, we archeologists can suggest directions for study in the years to come. Certainly we can help reveal the universals that confirm the unity of the human species within its magnificent variety, throughout its written and unwritten past.

In a turn-of-the-century photograph, a Makah hunter stands at the prow of an eight-man canoe to jab his harpoon into a breaching whale. Sealskin floats will buoy his line. By this method teams from Ozette captured whales in abundance.

N.G.S. PHOTOGRAPHER BRUCE DALE

COTTON COULSON

DAVID GRANT NOBLE

Growth rings of certain trees provide archeologists with information on past climatic conditions and with dates. During a drought, such a tree—especially conifers like the Douglas fir above—adds a narrow ring each year; with ample rain, it adds a thicker one. Dendro-chronologists, scientists who study tree rings, match these growth patterns from tree to tree, to establish chronological sequences. In the Southwest, tree rings yield dates accurate to the year for as early as 322 B.C. They provide a check on other methods such as radiocarbon analysis or newer techniques with margins of error as yet uncertain.

Animal remains, discarded by many archeologists in earlier days, can supply varied information. Bones of extinct species, or of those that live in particular habitats, can help determine environments long since changed. Remains of butchered game animals give an insight into human diets; but such factors as ease of hunting, or unknown food taboos, may make these a misleading sample. Thus the remains of micro-fauna—small creatures like shrews or field mice—assume importance as reliable clues to natural conditions in the past. Above, the skull of an eastern wood rat suggests temperate climate. Identifying tiny remains of this sort taxes the best resources of paleozoologists.

Plant remains aid in the reconstruction of past climates and cultures. The ratio of tree pollen to pollen from other plants suggests to a paleo-botanist the extent of forests at a given period. Palynologists can trace the varying abundance of fossil pollens through time and thus recognize changes from dry to humid or from hot to cold conditions. The presence of seed hulls from sunflowers (above) in a trash heap could indicate their role in the diet of a Southwestern people. Corn pollen or cobs, or the remains of squash and beans, would point to a village's degree of reliance on farming.

Make Use of It

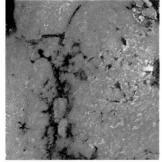

Nuclear physics today offers new resources for archeology. For example, raw turquoise like the sample above from a Zuñi pueblo ranked as a precious item in the ancient Southwest. A technique called neutron-activation analysis lets specialists identify trace elements in turquoise samples and thereby pinpoint the place of origin. Turquoise at the ancient Snaketown site, in Arizona, turned out to come from mines 190 miles away in California, not from prehistoric mines much closer by. A new method of dating minerals containing uranium, fission-track analysis, might show when fire heated a granite boulder on an ancient hearth.

Like many other small animals, snails live in narrowly limited habitats. Their remains indicate details of bygone micro-environments. Moreover, when mollusk shells fossilize, the amino acids they contain undergo a change called racemization. Delicate new methods of chemical analysis can detect the extent of change and reveal the time elapsed since an organism died, thus establishing the age of the stratum in which the remains appear. The snail shell above, of the species Mesomphix inornatus, *represents specimens from the Meadowcroft rock shelter in Pennsylvania. Ages of these shells range from 9000 B.C. to the present.*

Obsidian, volcanic glass widely used as a raw material for prehistoric tools, has a built-in clock that archeologists can read. Freshly worked or broken obsidian surfaces absorb moisture from the soil or the atmosphere at a determinable rate. This absorption, called hydration, slowly forms a denser layer where the glass breaks in minute parallel fractures. This layer alters the character of light passing through it in distinctive ways. By measuring this layer under a microscope, researchers can set limits for the time when an object took shape at a toolmaker's deft hands.

"I still think of it as 13th-century alchemy," says Dr. Robert Stuckenrath of his work in radiocarbon dating. At the Smithsonian Institution's Radiation Biology Laboratory, he burns an archeological sample of charcoal to convert it into carbon dioxide. The gas will contain carbon 14; its level of radioactivity will provide an approximate age for the sample. The "Merlin" nameplate on his door, a present from his wife, reflects his light-

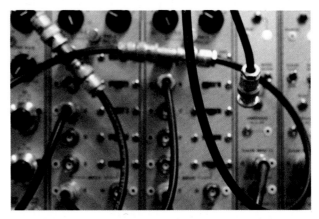

hearted outlook. His wizardry requires, in descending order, use of an electronic radiation counter (detail), a report by printout, and lab records.

THE SHELTERS AND THE CITY:

THE HERD OF BISON staggered in line against the 60-mile-an-hour wind of a late-autumn blizzard. The faces of the animals—nearly a hundred cows, yearlings, and calves—were matted with ice and snow. Calves struggled to keep up with their mothers. The bison were seeking refuge from the storm in the wooded bottomlands of the Arikaree River valley in the plains country of northeastern Colorado. The time was in the late Pleistocene, about 10,000 years ago.

In this same valley, hunters and their families huddled in shelters constructed of poles and bison hides. Their garments were cut from tanned hide stitched with sinew and worn hair-side-in. Fires eased the 40-below-zero cold as the people ate jerked bison meat or pemmican prepared with powdered jerky.

In one shelter, an old man worked a piece of stone—chert from a hundred miles away—into a delicately shaped spearpoint. He wore deer-hide pads to protect his hands from flying slivers. The sound of his antler hammer hitting the stone carried above the whine of the wind. Beside him lay other instruments of his craft: hammerstones, to break up lumps of chert; flakers, made of antlers from deer and elk, to work projectile points to razor sharpness.

Although nearly everyone in the band of seventy people could fashion tools and weapons out of stone, this man was one of a few who specialized in the art. Too old to hunt, he could still contribute to the band's well-being.

In another shelter, a group of hunters had gathered. They were short, power-fully built men who spoke in worried tones. Food was running low. Several of them trudged through the blizzard to consult the hunt chief—the shaman who organized bison hunts and was endowed with spiritual power to find and lure the herds. Confident of his magic, he may well have reassured them: "After the snow, we shall find meat. Soon. After the storm, we shall feast."

On a day of hunger, the wind calmed and the sun broke onto a silent landscape of sparkling white. The hunt chief sent young runners to scout for bison while he and the others tramped across a low hill, their breaths freezing in the icy air. They reached a shallow streambed filled with drifted snow. Here a line of trees and brush had acted as a snow fence, filling the gully. In the center of this draw, a tree trunk—with most of its branches lopped off—rose through the snow. This was the hunt chief's medicine pole, an instrument of ritual.

The people started trampling the snow on the south slope of the gully, packing it to make a slick ramp. The hunt chief approached the medicine pole, uttering incantations. From the branches that remained, he hung offerings, among them a tiny spear tipped with a stone point and a small flute made from an antler. A wolflike young animal was killed with a swift smash of stone upon its skull. The carcass was dismembered near the pole—another offering.

Soon the runners returned with word that a bison herd was moving through the valley to the southeast. A slight breeze blew from the northwest. Several hunters

FOUR ANCIENT SOCIETIES

followed the runners back, circling down-wind so the herd would not get their scent. Then they came up behind the bison and let themselves be seen. The animals trotted away warily.

Meanwhile other hunters, armed with spears and spear-throwers, had concealed themselves around the draw. Women, children, and older men had spread out from the ramp in two diverging lines. They were hiding behind mounds of snow.

As the bison approached this human funnel, the men behind them began shouting. The animals rushed forward — people sprang up behind the snow mounds, yelling and waving bison skins. And now their prey stampeded. Up the slope they galloped, only to slide helplessly down the ramp and into the drift. More and more animals tumbled in, trampling and crushing those already floundering in the deep snow.

The hunters attacked swiftly. Shouts and screams and the bellows of dying bison filled the air. Within a few minutes, the carnage was over. Nearly a hundred animals lay dead.

Jubilant, the people gathered. Quickly, with sharp stone knives, the tongues and the hump meat — prized delicacies — were stripped from several of the bison. For an hour or so, the people feasted on raw meat. Then they set to work more methodically, two or three to a carcass, skinning, cutting and slicing, and smashing skulls to remove the brains.

Fires had been started to melt marrow from the bones, to smoke strips of meat

New Sites and New Evidence Illuminate the Lengthening Span of Prehistory

By LOUIS DE LA HABA

SANDSTONE TABLET FROM MONKS MOUND, CAHOKIA, ILLINOIS; POSSIBLY SHOWING AN EAGLE DANCER. 2 7/16 BY 3 9/16 INCHES.

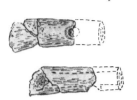

Man of magic, a Paleo-Indian shaman rides his medicine pole above a herd of stampeding bison. Hunters drive the animals into an enclosure of sticks and drifted snow to spear them. The scene takes place about 10,000 years ago. The shaman, credited with supernatural power to lure prey, waves a wand decorated with feathers. From the medicine pole hang offerings to the spirits — including a sacrificed vulture. A stone spearpoint in miniature and a broken flute made of deer antler (drawings, above) remained at the site near Wray, Colorado, and served as clues for archeologists who reconstructed the ancient hunt. At the Jones-Miller Paleo-Indian site, they have found the bones of some 300 bison killed and butchered between two Ice Age summers.

into jerky, and to ward off predators— mountain lions, huge grizzly bears of the plains, dire wolves.

A few days later, only piled-up bones remained. Again, in midwinter and in early spring, the hunt was re-enacted. In late spring, the band broke up. Family groups scattered with their few possessions. They would meet again in autumn.

Is this fiction? Is it absolute fact? Neither. It is a hypothetical reconstruction of past events based on the best archeological methods available today.

Visit the kill site with me as it existed until the autumn of 1975 on the ranch of Mr. and Mrs. Robert B. Jones, Jr., south of Wray, Colorado. And listen, as I did, to Dr. Dennis J. Stanford of the Smithsonian Institution, who directed excavations here for three seasons.

Over the centuries the Arikaree River has changed its course slightly, and the old draw has filled with sediment to become a mound in one of Mr. Jones's grainfields. In 1972, he wanted to extend one of his spray-irrigation systems, but the mound was in the way. He began to level it with earth-moving machinery and ran into the bone bed beneath the topsoil.

"At first I thought it was just a bunch of old cow bones," he told me. "But then I found some stone points."

He stopped work and told Mr. Jack Miller, a former anthropology instructor at Colorado State University. Preliminary excavation soon convinced Mr. Miller that he had an important discovery—a similar site about a hundred miles to the south, excavated by Dr. Joe Ben Wheat, had shed considerable light on Paleo-

Indian summer hunting strategy. The news reached Dr. Stanford; and the Smithsonian, with support from the National Geographic Society, decided to conduct a major excavation.

This accidental find reminded me of events in 1908 in Wild Horse Arroyo, near Folsom, New Mexico. There a black cowboy named George McJunkin noticed unusually large bones in the arroyo wall. He, too, reported what he had seen. At this site archeologists later excavated what were then the earliest Paleo-Indian artifacts in the United States: the famous Folsom points, clear evidence of man's antiquity in the New World.

When Dr. Stanford's crew of twenty-five students descended on the ranch, Mr. Jones generously provided a water supply, electricity, sanitary facilities, and two trailers. Excavations continued through 1975, far longer than he had expected. Although he was out several acres of productive land, he didn't mind. "I just thought it was worth doing," he told me.

I reached the site in time for dinner with Dr. Stanford and some of the crew. I cut my venison steak with a stone-flake knife, a copy of one of the Paleo-Indian tools, and it worked better than any steak knife I've ever used.

Late into the night, I talked with Dr. Stanford. He cautioned me that he had not drawn any final conclusions, and he told the story of the bison hunt. I kept wondering: "How can we know so much from a jumbled pile of 40,000 bones and fewer than a hundred and fifty stone tools, most of them broken?"

"The size of the herd we get from bone

bones in the wall of a washed-out arroyo. His find led to a momentous discovery in 1927: projectile points proving that Ice Age hunters lived in the New World some 10,000 years ago — 7,000 years earlier than experts had believed. One point lay between ribs of a large extinct bison.

counts," he explained, "and bones also give the sex of the animals.

"We can tell age from the teeth, the stage of eruption and the wear patterns. By looking at the teeth of the juveniles, we can see that some were older than others. And since we know that bison calves are born within a short period in the spring, we can deduce that they were killed at different times — younger ones in late fall and older ones in early spring."

How do we know what people wore? "A lot of that is speculation, but we have found bone awls and needles from other sites of about the same period." People with needles would stitch skins together to make snug clothing. "They must have," Dr. Stanford said emphatically. "There's just no way you're going to survive a Pleistocene winter draped in a loose-fitting bison robe."

The climate? "Well, this was not very long after the Wisconsin Ice Age, so we know it was much colder then and there was more snow. Even today it gets colder than all get-out."

The actual date? "Through carbon-14 analysis of the bones and charcoal."

I was curious about the vegetation. How could you know where trees may have stood when none grow there today? "By reconstruction of habitats from animal remains such as snail shells. Certain snails live in leaf litter, others in decaying logs, others under the roots of trees or in grass or in water. That is, snails are relatively habitat-specific; so are a lot of other little critters, like voles and frogs.

"We're identifying all the different snail shells we've found in this area and plotting

them like a topographic map. We can superimpose the habitats of other animals — animals that liked to live around fallen-down trees, or to burrow in dead-leaf mulch. It's plugging in very nicely, and gives us a picture of the ecology 10,000 years ago."

On the number of people, Dr. Stanford grew especially cautious: "That's tricky. We can make estimates from the amount of meat available from each kill. But if they had dogs, it would throw the whole thing off — dogs can eat a lot of meat. Still, the number of animals killed indicates a fairly large group."

And the number of flint workers? "The points are all of the same type, a type we call Hell Gap. But slight variations in manufacturing techniques cluster into several groups, so we can deduce there were only a few craftsmen. We haven't found the waste chips; but tiny flakes at the kill site indicate where tools were resharpened as they got dull."

I asked about the details of the bison hunt. "We can reconstruct that by comparison from historic times — what we call ethnographic analogy. Among the last Indians to hunt bison on foot were the Assiniboin and Cree of the northern prairies. Often they built impoundments of log posts and brush, or they used such formations as box canyons or steep-sided gullies. We haven't found anything like that, so we think our hunters used snow-drifts in the draw. We do have records of snow ramps — the Cree would slick them down with water."

When he told me about the hunt chief, he grinned. "That's one of the most inter-esting aspects. After the '74 season I read a dissertation by George Arthur from the University of Calgary. It had a good description of the Assiniboin hunt chief's role, how the medicine pole was set up, and how meat-eating birds were sacrificed.

"In '75 we got a big surprise. We found a postmold — the filled-in remains of a posthole — right in the middle of the draw! And that's where we found the little projectile point, which was too small for use on a spear. The antler flute was in the area, too. And that's also where we found the dismembered canid, either a dog or a wolf, with its skull crushed. The body had been deliberately butchered.

"This, to me, is really exciting. It shows a continuity of religious tradition going back 10,000 years."

As the night grew old, the wind came up and the temperature plummeted. My tent shook and flapped. I snugged down into a sleeping bag, and went to sleep thinking of the Pleistocene winter. Who were these people of so long ago, and how did they get here?

Archeologists call them Paleo-Indians. Their ancestors may have used the Bering land bridge, although even today it can be possible to walk from America to Asia when the sea freezes in winter. Some students of prehistory have proposed much earlier crossings than the late Pleistocene, as far back as 100,000 years. But among specialists the evidence for this view is generally considered tenuous.

Dates of about 27,000 years ago, based on carbon-14 analysis of bone implements at a site called Old Crow Flats in the Canadian Yukon, have some acceptance. But

conceivably these tools were made from bone already old. There are dates of 23,000 years ago from Tlapacoya, Mexico, based on an obsidian blade found under a log. But until recently, the earliest widely accepted date for man in North America was about 10,000 years ago, determined from three human skulls and associated animal remains at the Marmes rock shelter in the State of Washington.

Comparable evidence from Fell's Cave, at the tip of South America, gives dates of the same age. Within a thousand-year margin for error, how would people have traveled ten thousand miles?

Researchers on both sides of the Bering Strait continue to work on the problem. Recently a Soviet archeologist, Y. A. Mochanov, reported on excavations near Siberia's Aldan River. He suggested that "Proto-Americanoids" crossed over into Alaska about 25,000 years ago. Such a date would obviously allow time for people to move throughout the Americas.

The first "pioneers" did not enter the New World with what archeologist H. Marie Wormington has called "a Patagonia

or bust sort of attitude." They couldn't have known what new land lay beyond the next icefield; they must have adjusted their movements to those of game. All things considered, the exploration of two continents must have taken a long time.

With these thoughts in mind, I flew to Pennsylvania a few weeks later to meet Dr. James M. Adovasio of the University of Pittsburgh. Using some of the most sophisticated techniques known to archeology, he and Dr. Joel Gunn and other associates had obtained conclusive proof of human presence in western Pennsylvania at least 16,000 years ago.

Their site, fifty road miles southwest of Pittsburgh, is the Meadowcroft rock shelter. This is a natural recess in a sandstone cliff above Cross Creek, a tributary of the Ohio River.

As we drove there, Dr. Adovasio explained the significance of the site. "From the lowest levels to the surface—as we found it in 1973—we have an unbroken record from Paleo-Indian times to the present. On the surface, some of the first things we found were beer cans and a junkie's hypodermic needle; at the lowest levels, we have fire pits that are 16,000 to perhaps 19,000 years old. That's quite a cultural sequence!"

"What do these dates tell you?"

"Well, they tell me that the dates from Old Crow Flats are probably right."

We parked near a bridge over Cross Creek and, in the rain, climbed fifty feet up a steep slope. Excavation had ended for the season; a shed with a slanting roof protected the dig against winter. Inside, in the glare of floodlamps, our voices intrud-ed into the millenary silence of the damp and shadowy grotto.

Thousands upon thousands of years past, it had been much larger; the over-hanging roof had extended farther toward the creek. But huge portions had fallen in three cataclysmic episodes: one about 12,000 years ago, a second about 7,000 years ago, a third near the beginning of the Christian era. And the sandstone had eroded grain by grain through the action of wind, water, and freezing and thawing. These grains had been deposited on the shelter floor, layer upon layer, sealing and protecting the evidence for distinct periods of time.

The techniques of stratigraphy, of course, are based on the principle that objects found deeper are usually older than those closer to the surface. (Disturbances caused by earthquakes, burrowing animals, human projects, or other factors may complicate matters.)

Excavations at Meadowcroft were far from complete, but I could see the strata clearly in the east wall—outlines of hearths, bits of charcoal, fallen rock. I gazed into a deep trench at the outer edge of the shelter, where the earliest finds had been made. It was an enormous hole in time, down into sterile layers 28,000 years old.

The earliest cultural materials found to date have been hearths, worked stone tools, and stone flaking debris. Later levels, dated at about 16,000 years old, yielded stone blades, with other tools and more debris. Dr. Adovasio described these as "Siberian—looking like the stuff you get over there 18,000 to 20,000 years ago. Our blades aren't quite as sophisticated as

evidently served ritual purposes; the larger tipped a hunter's deadly spear. Both came from the Jones-Miller site. The style takes its name from a site found earlier in Wyoming.

the Siberian forms, but they are blades, no question about that."

The Meadowcroft archeologists have removed 228 metric tons of sediment. "We used nothing larger than a trowel," Dr. Adovasio said; "some of the crew use straight pins. Every bit of dirt has been put through screens, or a flotation process with water or hydrogen peroxide to recover very small bones and seeds and microscopic chipping debris and other minute particles. We have somewhere between two and three million bits of data—now, that would range from an unbroken artifact to a single seed or husk.

"This entire mass of information has been computerized. In fact, we have a computer terminal here in the shelter.

"Working with us are botanists, climatologists, geologists, geochemists, soil scientists, zoologists, and a whole heap of other folks. We're trying to extract as much information as we can.

"Our initial aim, of course, was to establish the chronological sequence—without that you know nothing. When we started, by the way, there were only 18 or 20 radiocarbon dates from all of western Pennsylvania, and that's a pretty big hunk of land. Now we have well over a hundred."

What about those earliest dates? "At first we were skeptical, but they were corroborated by a series of other carbon-14 dates in the same range and also by amino-acid analysis of snail shells.

"All living organisms contain amino acids, which have two forms: a left-handed, or L-isomer, and a right-handed, or D-

(Continued on page 58)

At the Jones-Miller site, workers clear overburden using brushes and
dental picks while surveyors check elevation to assure precise records.
Left on earthen pedestals, bison bones get maximum exposure for
photography and mapping. Crewman Mike Toft hoses dirt through
fine-mesh screens that act as sieves for microfossils such as snail shells
and for tiny flint flakes, residue of knives resharpened over the kills.

As the Paleo-Indian hunters butcher the cows
and calves they slaughtered, dire wolves — larger
than the modern species — rip apart the carcass of
a cow. Archeologists determined the sex and age of
the bison from details of skulls and teeth. Seen

from above, the mandible or lower jaw of the adult female (left) is thinner than that of the male. The state of tooth eruption, measured in profile, indicates the maturity of the animal; for calves born in spring, it gives proof of a kill in winter.

With a simple device a hunter achieves a mighty thrust.
Working like a lever, a spear-thrower — or atlatl — adds
power to the human arm, sending a stone-tipped
spear into flight. Dr. Stanford's throwing action becomes

vividly clear in this unique night-time photograph made possible by strobe lights triggered in sequence. The spear rises, then assumes a flat trajectory as it leaves the thrower. Despite the flashing lights, Dr. Stanford—a self-taught and experienced hunter—scored a direct hit on a four-inch-diameter target forty yards away.

Details, from left: atlatl, foreshaft with stone point, and main shaft; foreshaft joining main shaft; and spear loaded in throwing position. The atlatl copies an Eskimo type used until recently.

Near a melting ice sheet in western
Pennsylvania—its limits
determined by geologists—Paleo-
Indians of 16,000 years ago
butcher an elk. Stone tools used

by these wandering Ice Age hunters, a knife and two scrapers, provide evidence of their life in this region. Archeologists recently excavated the artifacts at the Meadowcroft rock shelter, some 75 miles to the south.

isomer. When alive, organisms have only L-isomers; but after they die, the isomers flop over to the right-handed type at a determinable rate. It's possible to tell the age of an organism from the proportion of right- and left-handed isomers. Because the amino-acid dates nearly duplicated our oldest carbon-14 dates, we feel confident about them."

Rain was still falling, and I asked Dr. Adovasio to describe conditions during those earliest times. "Remember, the ice sheet was just up the road a piece—about 75 miles north of here. Cross Creek runs east to west, so anyone or anything going either toward the Ohio or to eastern Pennsylvania had to pass through here or along parallel drainages.

"A small band of folks—maybe eight or ten people—going after elk or caribou is naturally going to use a shelter like this one. But no one stayed for long, because once they had collected the edible plants and hunted out the immediate area, they'd have to move on.

"As to what the people would be doing: Some would be gathering berries and seeds. Others would be hunting, or cutting and drying meat. If you had an old geezer around who happened to be 40—probably twice as old as he ought to be and still be living—he'd still be doing something useful, making projectile points or traps."

All lines of evidence suggest that the heaviest use of the shelter occurred from about 2000 B.C. to A.D. 300. For the Paleo-Indian period, say the excavators, evidence is still too incomplete to support any generalizations; but the availability of plant foods may well have dictated

visits to the site. After about 8500 B.C., fragments of eggshells from migratory waterfowl indicate springtime occupation, while the presence of seeds and nuts that mature in autumn point to reoccupation then.

Like the Jones-Miller site, Meadowcroft survived intact partly through chance but mainly because its importance was recognized. If a coal seam in the cliff had been worth exploiting, the shelter might not be there today. And if Albert and Delvin Miller, who own the property, had not understood its potential, the site might never have been reported and excavated. Thanks to them, the time perspectives of archeology in eastern North America have been greatly expanded.

Whatever the time span in question, archeology is, as Robert F. Heizer and John A. Graham have defined it, "the anthropology of the dead." Unlike their colleagues who deal directly with the living, archeologists are usually restricted to analyzing material remains. These may be scant indeed. Yet, as that reflective scientist Loren Eiseley has written, an artifact is a "humanly touched thing." It may suggest aspects of culture beyond the technological, or lend itself to the testing of precise hypotheses about the people who made it.

In the very center of Nevada—as stark and desolate and strangely beautiful a landscape as one could wish to see—I visited a dig where just such studies were in progress. The site was a rock shelter in the Monitor Valley, one of many valleys that run roughly north and south between ranges of the Great Basin. Sagebrush and

abounded in game, fish, berries, and nuts: food for man from Paleo-Indian times.
A team from the University of Pittsburgh, under Dr. James M. Adovasio, exposed these
tagged layers that represent some 14,000 years of human activity. Dark layers mark
living floors; a reddish area called a lens shows the location of prehistoric fires.

sand, hot springs and alkali flats mark the valley floors. On the slopes, juniper and piñon grow in profusion; and near sweet, cold running streams there are stands of quaking aspen. I spent several days here with Dr. David Hurst Thomas of the American Museum of Natural History in New York City and his crew of professional and student archeologists.

Grants from the museum, Educational Expeditions International (EEI) of Belmont, Massachusetts, and the National Geographic Society have supported the work. Dr. Thomas has been digging at Gatecliff since 1970. The earliest levels so far explored go back some 8,000 years. But early dates are not what Dr. Thomas is after. He wants to learn how people wrested a living from this land and why they came to Gatecliff.

Nature has lent a generous hand, for sediments brought in by flooding and by the wind have sealed in each occupation level, or "living floor." There are at least 14 such floors, generally separated by thick layers of sediments and spared the immense rockfalls of Meadowcroft. Thus it is possible to expose an entire living floor. From the nature and distribution of artifacts, hearths, plant and animal remains, and other items, archeologists can reconstruct a picture of what was happening during any particular occupation.

Some levels are so thin that Dr. Thomas thinks the shelter was used only sporadically. Perhaps hunters who had conducted an antelope drive in the valley brought their game to the shelter for butchering. Large concentrations of heavy grinding stones might indicate a women's task

J. M. ADOVASIO

In Nevada's stark Monitor Valley, excavations at Gatecliff rock shelter illuminate lifeways of a nomadic people who subsisted on the meager resources of the Great Basin: piñon nuts, ricegrass seeds, fish, birds, and small game. The exposed level dates from about 1500 B.C. Rock art in another shelter suggests a prehistoric tradition centered on hunting magic. Overleaf: In a cloud of desert dust, Rosalie Dvorák fine-screens bucketloads of dirt for small objects diggers may have missed.

group engaged in grinding piñon nuts.

"A lot of archeologists think that Indians preferred to live in caves," Dr. Thomas remarked. "I don't think that's true. It's the archeologists who prefer caves. In dry regions there's good preservation of materials such as basketwork, snares, and sandals. Cave stratigraphy tends to stack up nicely, too. But I think the Indians chose sites for other reasons—around here they preferred the tops of ridges."

The most recent Indian inhabitants of the area were the Shoshoni, studied in the 1930's by the eminent anthropologist Julian H. Steward. They were hunters and gatherers who moved about according to the season. Piñon nuts were their staple, supplemented by ricegrass seeds, waterfowl, antelope, and small game.

Dr. Thomas used Steward's data for a computerized testing of how archeological materials fit in with facts of Shoshoni lifeways. Into the computer went such information as types of tools used, subsistence activities, seasonality of food resources, long- and short-term climatic changes, locations of piñon-juniper belts, of lakes, of ricegrass fields, and many other factors.

"We simulated a band of Indians, moving around the land for a thousand years, using the local resources. Every time they'd move, we'd have them drop tools appropriate to whatever they were doing.

"At the end we had, on paper, a thousand years' worth of artifacts spread out over all the lifezones. The computer predicted the types and proportions of artifacts we should find in different areas if the prehistoric peoples lived just like the Shoshoni. We gridded off a map of the Reese River valley—that's just a couple of valleys over—that the computer had generated; then we surveyed the countryside to see what we would find. About 85 percent of the predictions were correct.

"I think the reason is that this environment has very little leeway, and that the way people lived a hundred years ago was not much different from what people did five thousand years ago."

He told me how an explorer named J. H. Simpson had come upon a startled Shoshoni in 1859: "The Indian was sitting there with a string of 27 pack rats and one lizard. That was his dinner.

"Now, one year when I was working on my master's thesis, I was collecting animals—we had to get a type collection of bones so we could identify what we found. I tried eating everything, including pack rats and lizards. You know, they're not bad. You could really acquire a taste for them. What we have here is something more or less universal, a group of people trying to exploit every resource their ecology offers."

The work at Gatecliff continues to illuminate the lifeways of the Shoshoni and their predecessors. It has also produced a mystery. This is a concentration of nearly 500 limestone tablets of fairly uniform size—no larger than the palm of the average hand. They have been incised with various patterns, some seemingly random, others more geometric, others with figures vaguely suggestive of animals.

Dr. Thomas's wife, Trudy, is studying these, looking for possible consistencies in workmanship and motifs. She has reached no conclusions yet as to their

nature or purpose. They could have been associated with hunting magic; they may even have recorded periodic events.

Such tablets are rare; few sites yield more than two or three. Their profusion at Gatecliff raises intriguing questions about the spiritual life of this ancient desert people.

Much more abundant evidence, from much later in time, informs us about the people who created the largest, most influential city north of Mexico in pre-Columbian days. This was Cahokia, which had a superbly strategic location near the confluences of the Mississippi, Missouri, and Illinois Rivers.

Specifically, it flourished in the rich environment known as the American Bottoms, a 175-square-mile area on the eastern side of the Mississippi River. Its beginnings extend backward beyond A.D. 800; but it reached its population peak between 1050 and 1250. It may have had as many as 38,000 inhabitants, with a stratified society headed by a chief or a king. It was clearly the leading power in the American Bottoms; and its influence may have extended northward to the Aztalan site in Wisconsin, a community that probably controlled copper sources.

The civilization that produced Cahokia was a part, if not the very origin, of what archeologists call the Mississippian tradition. In late prehistory its influence spread through much of the eastern United States. And the unfolding story of Cahokia illustrates the kind of studies that focus on cultural change.

Here scale becomes evidence in its own right. Cahokia is arranged around Monks

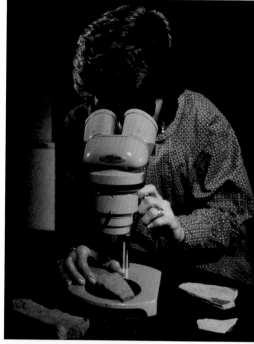

Puzzle of Gatecliff—500 incised and enigmatic limestone tablets. Trudy Thomas, wife of Gatecliff director David Hurst Thomas, examines one of them with a zoom microscope; the enlargement above shows what she sees. The tablets may have had religious significance, she says, but as yet no one knows for certain.

Waiting out a rare rainstorm at Gatecliff, about 1500 B.C., members of a hunter-gatherer band catch up on maintenance work. One man knaps flint for tools; another fashions a

rabbit net from plant fibers; women roast piñon nuts over a fire. Waste flakes around this rock
as exposed at the dig, rabbit bones, and an ancient hearth supplied the basis for this painting.

Mound, an earthen flat-topped monument that has no equal in size north of the Pyramid of the Sun in Teotihuacan and the great pyramid at Cholula, in Mexico. Monks Mound is estimated to contain 21,690,000 cubic feet of soil, and to have taken three centuries to build.

Once there may have been 120 mounds in Cahokia. Fewer than 65 still keep their original shape. Railroad rights-of-way, highways, stores, housing developments, fast-food facilities, gas stations, and even a drive-in movie theater have encroached upon the site. The Illinois state park system, however, has reclaimed the main portion, "downtown Cahokia."

Both amateur and professional archeologists have been busy here for nearly a century and a half. Large-scale studies began in the 1960's, with a program involving several universities and the Illinois State Museum. One of these groups is led by Dr. Melvin L. Fowler of the University of Wisconsin-Milwaukee.

I paid him a visit one cold blustery day, and he showed me some of the treasures recovered from a single burial mound: thousands of conch-shell beads from the Gulf of Mexico; rolled sheets of copper from near Lake Superior; artfully chipped arrowheads from Oklahoma, Arkansas, and Tennessee; mica from North Carolina. "Such an extensive range of materials attests to Cahokia's economic power and far-flung trade relations," he said.

This structure, Burial Mound 72, held the remains of at least three important personages who died at different times. "Perhaps a father, a son, and a grandson — that's pure speculation — but certainly the complexity of the burials indicates a tremendous status," Dr. Fowler told me. The immense amount of grave goods implies members of a chiefly or aristocratic lineage, but the evidence goes further.

Bundle burials — bundles of disjointed bones — suggest that remains of lesser members of the lineage had been kept in a charnel house for interment at the death of a chief. Skeletons indicate funeral sacrifice. One burial grouping contained the remains of more than 50 young women, with four males whose heads and hands had been cut off.

"You just don't do away with that many people unless the person who died was someone very important," Dr. Fowler remarked as we turned to other topics.

On a well-worn map, he showed me the complexity of the site. Several areas of dotted circles represented "woodhenges," circles of wooden poles. With much caution, the investigators have suggested that these circles may have been used for observations of the sun, to determine the solstices and equinoxes and thus to define a calendar year.

Flat-topped mounds, concern with death and human sacrifice, study of sun and moon and planets and stars — all reminded me of Mesoamerican sites I had visited in Mexico, Guatemala, and Belize. Was there some connection?

"Many people believe there was," he replied. "Certainly, I don't deny that some Mesoamerican influences may have reached here, but on the archeological evidence, I think Cahokia was largely a native development."

On other maps, he traced for me the

growth of population in the American Bottoms, from a small group of scattered settlements, through the establishment of villages and towns, to the emergence of Cahokia as a dominant economic center.

Then he summed up explanations for Cahokia's ascendancy: the natural productivity of the fertile soils; the development of new strains of corn; the change from digging sticks to the far more efficient hoe; the access to and control of a wide variety of goods by river-borne trade.

By the late 14th century, construction at Cahokia stopped and the population began to decline. Eventually the city was abandoned, visited only occasionally by local Indians who came to bury their dead.

Why Cahokia waned is one of the questions that cannot be answered simply. Again, I am reminded of events far away: the abandonment of the huge city of Teotihuacan about A.D. 750, the collapse of the Classic Maya civilization some 200 years later. Even today, within the lifetimes of many of us, empires have disappeared and great cities have faltered.

For Cahokia, the possibility remains that satellite communities became powerful in their own right, took over the trade networks, and denied Cahokia access to the resources that created its wealth. We may find, as Dr. Fowler has written, another stage in the development of complex societies, "a reintegration and spreading out into smaller socio-political groups."

Indeed, among smaller groups the heritage of Cahokia was not utterly lost; and that story comes not only from the buried goods of the dead but also in part from the words of the living.

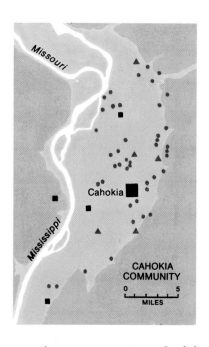

On the Mississippi River floodplain an empire grew and flourished. From the city of Cahokia (large square) rulers dominated lesser administrative and religious centers (small squares) which in turn controlled minor towns (triangles) and agricultural villages (circles). These fed and honored the reigning elite of the metropolis. Cahokia reached its zenith about A.D. 1250, with a population of some 38,000. At the height of its power, its influence extended over much of eastern North America.

8 INCHES, BEAK TO TAIL

Treasure of Cahokia's dead: Pottery and arrowpoints of masterly workmanship honored men of exalted rank. The wood-duck bowl has a hollow head that acts as a rattle; the beaver bowl shows the animal's sharp incisors. Supreme examples of the flintworker's art, the arrowheads formed part of three caches totaling more than 1,100 points found as burial offerings in a single mound, Mound 72. Other grave goods here number in the thousands; the variety of styles and materials reveal wide-ranging networks of trade. Not all Cahokia's people received such honors in death—classic evidence, to the archeologist, of a stratified social system.

10 INCHES, HEAD TO TAIL

ABOUT TWICE ACTUAL SIZE

NATIONAL GEOGRAPHIC PHOTOGRAPHER OTIS IMBODEN (BELOW AND UPPER RIGHT)

Seven miles from "downtown" Cahokia's flat-topped
Monks Mound, St. Louis's Gateway Arch rises
gleaming. Farming and suburban incursions—the
latter now on the wane—destroyed much of the old
Indian city. Illinois made the heart of the site a
state park in 1925. Above, archeologists on the first
terrace of Monks Mound remove backfill from a trench
covered over for protection between excavation seasons.

FROM THE WORDS OF THE

THAT SPRAWLING disturbed landscape always amazes me. When I visit Cahokia, I know that it is not alone, for many other sites within our borders testify to the accomplishments of the American Indian. But Cahokia is the grandest. It represents an unparalleled zenith in native American development.

I have walked a little of the central area, more than five square miles, roughly a fourth the size of Manhattan Island. I have climbed some of the great mounds not yet leveled for suburban development. I have made my way up Monks Mound, named for a Trappist community that settled here briefly in the early 1800's; it bulks to a height of one hundred feet, the largest mound in the United States.

"When you climb it," my friend George Stuart says truly, "you lose the sense of its moundness. It's like a mountain. It still dominates the suburbs coming in around it—it's still king."

Always the same questions strike eager students and jaded colleagues, alike bemused by their surroundings: What manner of people were these? How could they have done it? And to what purpose?

Difficult questions to address to those quiet mounds vacant of ancient life. Yet not impossible questions.

Archeology has already answered some of them. We know from soil textures and scraps of basketwork that the mounds were built basketload upon load. Tedious, dirty, long-sustained labor by untold thousands of people.

I have stood in the plazas, and considered the plan that distinguishes sites like Cahokia from earlier ones. These complex places reserved their highest points for temples and for the abodes of priest-kings; and this arrangement poses one of the most disputed questions in American archeology. Does it reflect an undocumented contact with the great civilizations of Mexico?

Perhaps the new technologies will bring us closer to all the answers we seek; and perhaps, too, the old manuscripts.

Investigation of the prehistoric past can be almost maddening, even at an unplundered site. Oh yes, we have our methods of transforming projectile points and potsherds into some pale image of the people who lived, but we still fall far short of understanding the hows and whys of ancient life.

As a graduate student at Yale in the mid-1960's I decided to write a dissertation on some of the late prehistoric peoples of Mississippi who were heirs in part of great Cahokia, hundreds of miles distant. Time and again I was frustrated. Only the sparse tokens of complex events could be brought forth from the ground.

It was then that the manuscripts began to fascinate me. Those yellowed and crackling pages. Those marvelous accounts of the early European explorations in North America, so fraught with adventure, so full of the excitement of discovery and conquest, and equally of disaster and perished expeditions.

And scattered throughout, casually interwoven in the stories, are details about the lives of the Indians that the data of archeology cannot begin to approach. For the first explorers found the Indian in his aboriginal state. They made their observa-

LIVING: THE INDIAN SPEAKS

tions firsthand, while we can observe only dust and dry bones. There was flesh on the bones then, and the cultures lived as well as the people.

Hernando de Soto, lieutenant to Francisco Pizarro in the conquest of Peru, newly appointed governor of the ill-defined realm of Florida, embarked on a great exploration of his new domain in May 1539. Four chronicles tell the story: a brief report for the King of Spain by an official named Luys Hernandez de Biedma; a narrative by Gonzalo Fernandez de Oviedo y Valdés, based on the diary kept by de Soto's secretary Rodrigo Ranjel; a longer one by a Portuguese known only as the Gentleman of Elvas; and a history compiled by Garcilaso de la Vega.

Each of these sources offers a different perspective. Biedma submits a factual account to justify the expenditure of time, money, and lives. Ranjel offers a plain, unvarnished description of day-to-day events. The Gentleman of Elvas gives a more elaborate history of the expedition, with details of Indian as well as Spanish personalities.

Garcilaso cannot write as an eyewitness, although he knew one of the survivors well and read memoirs by others. Yet he has a distinctive basis of insight. Son of a conquistador and an Inca princess, he spins a romantic tale of chivalry. He tells with equal sympathy of Spanish zeal and Indian valor—a quaint compound of medieval knight-errantry and Indian warfare.

In part because of these different objectives, these chronicles often disagree

Eyewitness Documents Gain New Authority From the Records of Archeology

By JEFFREY P. BRAIN, *Ph.D.*
Peabody Museum of Archaeology and Ethnology, Harvard University

on details. Garcilaso, lavish with figures, says the expedition had 1,000 men and 250 horses. Probably closer to the mark, Ranjel gives the force 570 men and 243 horses; Elvas, 600 men and 213 horses; Biedma, 620 men and 223 horses. Whatever the actual numbers, this was the largest and best-equipped expedition yet to set foot on American soil when it landed near Tampa Bay.

De Soto was a hard man, "much given," said a contemporary, "to the sport of hunting Indians." From the beginning he chose to adopt a policy of intimidation. The Indians had never seen a horse, and were terrified by the prospect of a figure half-man-half-beast. Often, as Garcilaso emphasized, the mere appearance of the cavalry would scatter determined parties of warriors. The Spanish were well aware of this, and the loss of a horse was accounted far more serious than the death of a mere foot soldier.

This military advantage was combined with an unscrupulous diplomacy. Such ruses as the kidnapping of chiefs were another alternative to battle.

The Indians were hunted, harassed, and finally harnessed to the cause, enslaved as porters and menials. Recalcitrant braves had a hand or a nose — or head — struck from the living flesh as an example to others. Many women were seized, said Ranjel, "and these not old nor the most ugly" because they were "desired both as servants and for foul uses and lewdness."

Thus de Soto fought his way along in a great perambulating journey to find wealth like that of the Incas. He was disastrously unsuccessful in this venture, though he pursued it mightily for three incredible years.

His general route is known. It traversed some 350,000 square miles of Indian domains, frequently and understandably hostile. From present-day Florida he went north through Georgia, the Carolinas, Tennessee; south through Alabama; north again through Mississippi, until he "discovered" the Mississippi River, his popular claim to fame.

Unfortunately, the exact point of discovery is unknown and, as a result, every river town between Memphis and Vicksburg claims that distinction. The reason is simple: The conquistadors themselves never knew exactly where they were. Their chroniclers made some effort to record the strange names of villages and "provinces," as pronounced by various interpreters; but identifying these places has baffled experts for decades.

There are rare exceptions. The "Mauvila" of Garcilaso or "Mabila" of Elvas were settled just north of modern Mobile, Alabama. But more often the vagueness and the discrepancies are so great that the people and places remain lost to us. As a senior colleague and dear friend, Philip Phillips, wrote in 1951, "a paleontologist with half a tooth has a better chance of reconstructing his animal."

Since 1939, however, the Peabody Museum has sponsored the Lower Mississippi Archaeological Survey. A number of organizations have taken a valued part, among them the National Geographic Society. This project has mapped thousands of sites, excavating many, and accumu-

lated hundreds of thousands of bits of evidence, mostly broken pottery.

Our preoccupation with potsherds has rendered us less than perfect, if not downright suspect, in the eyes of local beholders. Some have wondered what we were *really* after, while others simply think us crazy. One conversation among the workmen overheard by a member of the Survey many years ago included this:

"Them Northern fellers must be really crazy in the head. Here they come all the way down here and spend all that money, and spend months digging up all those little broken pieces of pottery; and when they get them, they cart them off to that little house in town where they wash them, clean them, and look at them awhile; and then they cart them all off to the town dump and throw them away!"

I should explain that in those days archeologists might discard some pieces: unmarked bits without decoration and without any useful details of shape, such as the thickness of a base or the curve of a rim. Today we even save those. For it is the lowly potsherd, more than anything

St. Louis loses a landmark, Big Mound, last and largest of more than seven at a satellite town of Cahokia. In 1852, grading for Broadway and Mound Streets exposes the inner structure; in 1869, workmen complete the demolition after a railroad bought the earth for roadbed. Old records give the original size—319 feet by 158 at the base, 34 feet high —but say little about the "relics" unearthed but no longer traceable.

as:vierã logo os indios pello rio
abaixo,saltaram em terra τ ao go
uernador diſſerã ɋ eram vaſſallos
de hũ gram señor ɋ Aquixo ſe cha
maua ɋ muitos pouos τ de muita
gente da outra parte do rio ſenbo
reaua que de ſua parte lhe faziã ſa
ber que ao outro dia elle cõ todos
os ſeus viria a ver ho ɋ ſua ſenbo
ria lhe mãdaua logo ho outro dia
veo ho caciɋ cõ duzẽtas almadias
cheas de indios cõ ſeus arcos τ fre
chas almagrados τ cõ grãdes pena
chos de penas brancas/τ de cores
muitos per hũa τ outra bãda cõ pa

else, that has provided the most dramatic breakthrough in our researches.

Painstaking sorting and prolonged study has discriminated complexes of these potsherds. Now we can place the sites they came from in time as well as in space. Analysis has revealed that some sites were occupied and abandoned too early for de Soto's visit, others settled too late. By this long winnowing-out process, a few sites among many have been identified with the de Soto dateline. These are the only candidates for those living villages described in the documents. Thus we have clarified some of the problems of de Soto's route.

I am confident that I have stood near where he first looked in awe at the greatest river he had ever seen: near Friars Point, in Coahoma County, Mississippi, not far from the city of Clarksdale.

I had the fun of visiting Clarksdale in the spring of 1974 — 433 years later, almost to the day — to tell the Mississippi Archaeological Association that the conquistadors had marched right through the area. Those ephemeral footsteps are as sacred as "Washington slept here" in other regions. Clarksdale enthusiastically welcomed the news. This was vindication for a modest stone monument hopefully erected fifty years earlier. (A local joke says the great bronze statue at the center of De Soto Park in Memphis has turned a brighter shade of green out of pure envy!)

As I drove into Clarksdale from the south, on U. S. 49, I could imagine the relief of that bedraggled army when it emerged from the dark backwater swamps infested with alligators and brooded over by stands of giant cypress dripping gauzy sweeps of Spanish moss.

In this sinister atmosphere the Spaniards had forced a march and descended upon the first of unsuspecting communities of a native chiefdom. On the site of Clarksdale in 1541 was a town with the exotically alliterative name of Quizquiz.

Quizquiz was the capital of a rich province inhabited by Indians now known as the Tunica. This town must have been a sort of mini-Cahokia. Archeological reports from the 1890's tell us it had at least six mounds, perhaps more; the largest supported the chief's house, and a great earthen embankment surrounded the whole. (The earthworks have long since been obliterated; and the modern city hall, county courthouse, and federal building — the administrative centers of today — stand within the old sacred precincts.)

"Relics of de Soto" have been sought and reported over the years: pieces of chain mail, halberds, swords. This hardware usually turns out to be French, English, or even American. De Soto's army sensibly held on to its weapons while it discarded nearly everything else. Lightweight trinkets that were standard gift items would be more likely clues to de Soto's visit. And a mound near Clarksdale contained some.

In a child's grave were some turquoise beads. To date this is the only known occurrence of turquoise at an Indian site east of the Mississippi. Alone, the beads would suggest a native trade route with the Southwest. But with them was found a distinctive little sheet-brass bell of Spanish origin; five other sites reasonably near

de Soto's route have yielded examples of the "Clarksdale bell." Apparently some Spaniard had acquired the turquoise, possibly from Hawikuh pueblo by way of Mexico, and brought it here.

De Soto's force paused at Quizquiz only long enough to note the fortresslike layout and the thousands of armed warriors gathering to test their courage. The army had dwindled, a score killed here, "13 or 14 men" and 57 horses there.... De Soto knew he could follow this great new river to the Gulf of Mexico and find his way back to Spanish dominions.

But he was a proud man, and to return with nothing to show for his endeavors would be ruin.

Then, apparent salvation floated down the river. The most detailed description is that of the Gentleman of Elvas:

"A great chief arrived, with two hundred canoes filled with men, having weapons. They were painted with ochre, wearing great bunches of white and other plumes of many colours, having feathered shields in their hands, with which they sheltered the oarsmen on either side, the warriors standing erect from bow to stern. The barge in which the great chief came had an awning at the poop, under which he sat; and the like had the barges of the other chiefs: and ... where the chief man sat, the course was directed and orders issued.... All came down together, and arrived within a stone's cast of the bank."

De Soto was walking along the bank, with his crossbowmen hidden. This chief, like others, made a flattering formal speech: "that he had come to visit, serve and obey him; for he had heard that he

Tunica Treasure: Trade links with Indians in present-day Minnesota brought this catlinite pipe to a chief's grave in a Louisiana village. The brass-and-rhinestone cross may have come from Father Antoine Davion, a missionary among the Tunica from 1699 to 1721. They did not adopt his faith; but the author believes they may have accepted this cross as a sparkling, exotic trinket.

Widow of the last Tunica chief, Mrs. Rose Pierite gazes from the door of her home in Marksville, Louisiana. Her husband, Chief Joseph Alcide Pierite, died in 1976; their son, Joe, Jr., of New Orleans, serves as chairman of the Tunica-Biloxi council. Bebe Barbry (above), one of seven Tunica still living in Marksville, receives a visit from his step-daughter. Below: selected items, Indian and European, of the Tunica Treasure, which included hundreds of metal utensils, firearms, and thousands of glass beads as burial gifts.

At first contact—with de Soto in 1541—the
Tunica lived in northern Mississippi, with their
capital at Quizquiz. They moved south to the
Yazoo River in the 17th century under pressure

was the greatest of lords, the most powerful on all the earth...."

De Soto tried to persuade him to come
ashore for a parley, hoping to take him
captive. The chief countered by ordering
up three barges loaded with fish and per-
simmon bread as a gift. Foiled, de Soto ordered the crossbowmen to fire. Although
five or six Indians were struck down, there
was no panic.

"They retired with great order, not one
leaving the oar, even though the one next
to him might have fallen.... These were
fine-looking men, very large and well
formed; and what with the awnings, the
plumes, and the shields, the pennons, and
the number of people in the fleet, it appeared like a famous armada of galleys."

This was extraordinarily high praise
from the usually arrogant Spaniards! Here
was no disorganized rabble, no savage ef-
frontery, but rather a most carefully mo-
bilized and formidable display of power
by a highly organized kingdom. Here, in
fact, was some reflection of great Cahokia
brought to vibrant life.

Such descriptions seemed wildly fanci-
ful to sound historians in the 19th century.
No Indian tribe, they assumed, could mus-
ter disciplined forces of this kind—surely
the chroniclers were giving their tale the
glamor of a novel, trying to make their
own exploits worthy of adventures in
Mexico or Peru!

Now we can say with confidence that
we should expect just such societies from
the archeological evidence—a town like
Quizquiz is no simple little village. We can
consult the manuscripts for the real sub-
stance they contain; this in turn brightens

and completes the pictures of archeological reconstruction. And sometimes, as in
this instance, the narrative has a convinc-
ing logic of its own.

If only a pale reflection of the Inca and
Aztec empires, the Indian armada was
enough encouragement for the dispirited
army. Once again, they became conquistadors. Power like this must have commen-
surate wealth to sustain it! This single
event was enough to keep them searching,
vainly, for another two years for the hidden riches of the land.

Unopposed, the Spaniards crossed the
river to explore the west country. Months
of wandering finally convinced them that
they would not find gold and gems, and
they turned back to the Mississippi with
the thought of escape.

Returning to the river, they entered the
greatest of all the 16th-century Indian
kingdoms, Quigualtam. Its seat of power
was probably at the immense Emerald
Mound in Adams County, Mississippi.

Apparently this arrival was a matter of
chance, but it offered one final opportunity to salvage a disaster. De Soto, mortally
sick, would need help to save his dwin-
dling army. The Gentleman of Elvas tells
how he sought it:

"De Soto sent a messenger to the chief,
Quigualtam, to say that he was the child of
the Sun, and whence he came all obeyed
him, rendering their tribute; that he be-
sought him to value his friendship, and to
come where he was; that he would be rejoiced to see him; and in token of love
and his obedience, he must bring him
something from his country that was in
most esteem there."

from Indian allies of the English; in 1706 they bypassed the homeland of their foes the Natchez to settle near their allies the French. Keen traders, they supported the French when colonial troops attacked the rebellious Natchez in 1730. They later moved west to Marksville, where a few descendants still live on tribal land.

This message contained the old arrogance of Spain, but it was answered in like kind. The messenger brought back this reply:

"As to what you say of your being the son of the Sun, if you will cause him to dry up the great river, I will believe you; as to the rest, it is not my custom to visit anyone, but rather all, of whom I have ever heard, have come to visit me, to serve and obey me, and pay me tribute, either voluntarily or by force: if you desire to see me, come where I am; if for peace, I will receive you with special goodwill; if for war, I will await you in my town; but neither for you, nor for any man, will I set back one foot."

Already ill, de Soto soon died "of melancholy." His survivors eventually fled for their lives downriver, pursued by the warriors of Quigualtam.

That experience discouraged further European exploration in the Mississippi Valley for nearly a century and a half. In the Southwest, expeditions from Mexico found new lands to rule—but again, no gold. Spain's fortunes waned, while the emerging powers of Great Britain and France began to focus on the North American continent. They established colonies along the eastern seaboard and then began a race for domination.

First to recognize the importance of the Mississippi Valley were the French. The individual most responsible was René Robert Cavelier, Sieur de la Salle. He left Canada in late summer, 1681, to follow the river to the Gulf of Mexico and plant the banner of Louis XIV at its mouth.

And en route, on March 26, 1682, he

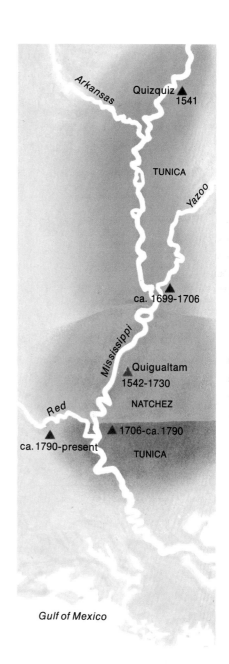

Gulf of Mexico

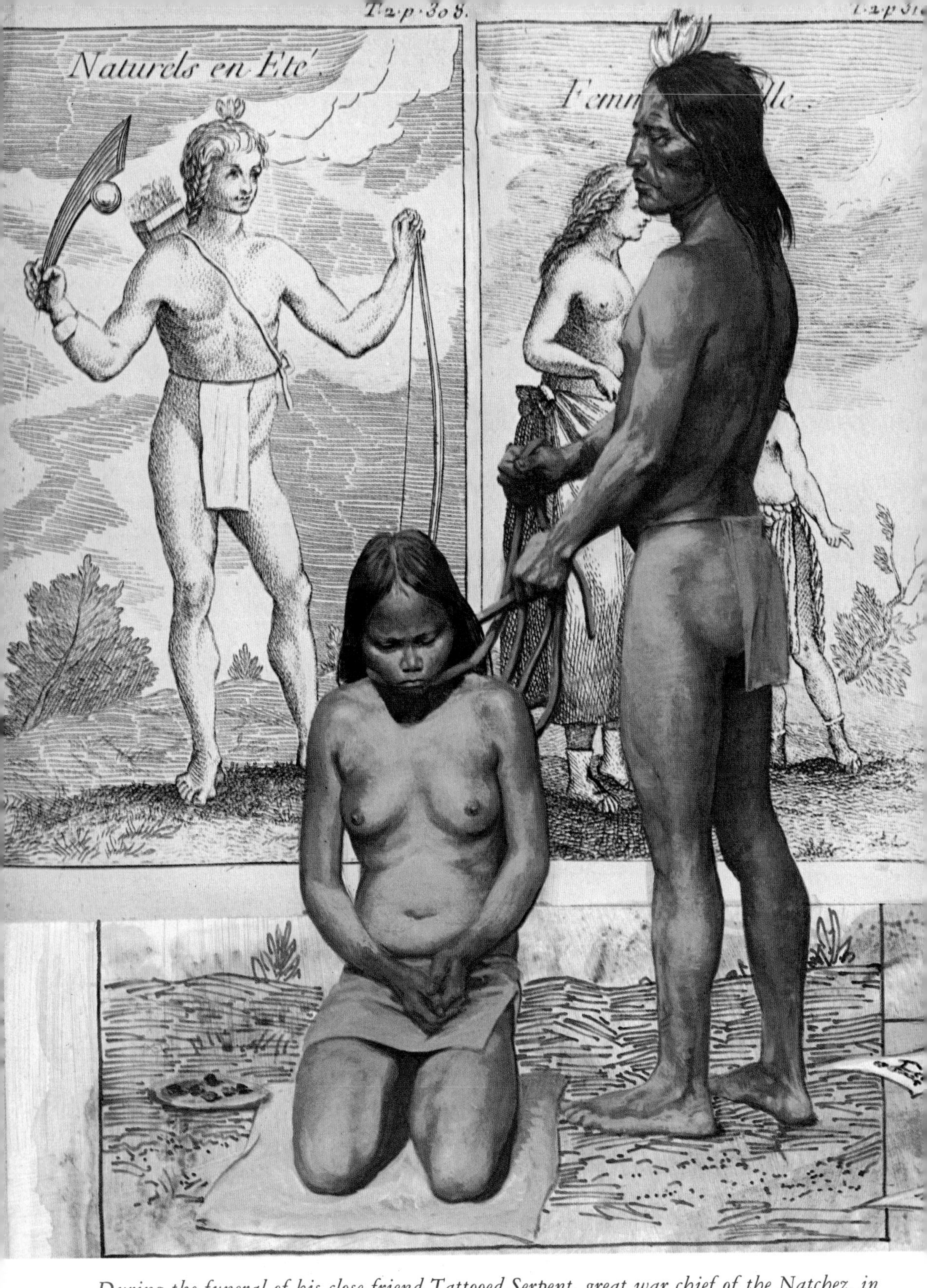
T.2.p.308.
Naturels en Eté.

During the funeral of his close friend Tattooed Serpent, great war chief of the Natchez, in 1725, French scholar-adventurer Antoine Le Page du Pratz records the ceremony. When the litter-bearers enter the temple, burial place of rulers, those who die in sacrifice give their

lives to join their chieftain "in the country of the spirits." Du Pratz sketched eight victims but wrote of ten, wives and retainers among them. He lived among the Natchez eight years, learning customs and beliefs; his renderings of summer costumes appear at upper left.

re-established contact with Quigualtam's people, later known as the Natchez. Apparently he saw the great Emerald Mound, mentioned as "a beautiful eminence."

But again, as so often, the old manuscripts fail us. They say little of this momentous event, only that the French received a kindly welcome. For details of Quigualtam, archeology is the last resort.

Emerald Mound ranks as one of the grandest earthen constructions by the late prehistoric Indians in North America; north of Mexico, only Monks Mound exceeds it. Its base covers more than seven acres. On this huge raised platform now stand two smaller mounds, one about 30 feet high—the temple site.

Inevitably this jewel of Mississippi's past has attracted attention. Since early in the 19th century, Emerald has been dug by the idly curious and the dedicated dilettante. The professional came late to the scene. Undoubtedly, many finds went unreported—possibly splendid ones.

In a rare instance of record, some sixty years ago a gentleman of Natchez, Vincent Perrault, unearthed a series of spectacular limestone pipes carved in grotesque man-animal forms. These pipes, of exceptional esthetic quality, were ceremonial regalia, a reminder of the Quigualtam reported by de Soto's men.

No direct evidence of European visitors had ever been recorded from Emerald, perhaps because no one looked for appropriate items, perhaps because such fleeting contacts rarely leave substantial remains. The Lower Mississippi Survey made one more effort. Emerald is too important to be ignored and the de Soto and La Salle expeditions are too exciting to be forgotten.

Under my direction, a Survey team excavated at the summit of the mound during the summer of 1972. We did not find the artifacts we hoped for. Not a single bead or bell or other exotic trade item. But we did document further some aspect of a great and vanished people.

A deep trial hole proved that this vast construction had been completed during a relatively brief period. Digging by hand helps one appreciate the scope of the ancient work—labor that must have consumed the energy of several generations.

And at the summit we found the graves of those personages whose last treasure had been taken by Perrault. Before us lay the bones of the people who had caused this astonishing monument to be built. Such achievements required skill in engineering, of course, but more in social management.

In prehistory the Southwest excelled in architecture; its buildings are the most sophisticated within our borders. But its societies were comparatively simple and egalitarian. The Southeast was the region of complex social organization; and this was a special attribute of the Quigualtam, or Natchez.

"The most civilized of native tribes are the Natchez." So said men of all stations as the French developed their hold on the Mississippi Valley. Since they considered their own the most civilized nation in Europe, this was high tribute, indeed.

Unlike other tribes, the Natchez had commoner and noble classes. The former were called Stinkards (but not to their

faces). The aristocracy had three ranks: in ascending order, Honored, Nobles, and Suns. The sacred paramount chief was entitled the Great Sun, which suggested a direct comparison to Louis XIV, *le Roi-Soleil,* the Sun King. Good sense itself, remarked an approving Frenchman, had taught these people that a great prince should wear a crown of white plumes on a red diadem—"very pleasing to the sight."

Thus the French were both drawn to the Natchez and ready to see them as rivals. By the early 1700's, French trading posts and plantations had begun to exert pressure on the sacred grand village, represented today by the Fatherland site on the outskirts of the city of Natchez.

Fatherland is a modest site. There are only three small mounds, a scant ten acres of ceremonial ground. The Natchez themselves numbered only a few thousand souls in 1700, a mere remnant of the population suggested in the de Soto narratives and revealed by the archeology of Quigualtam. What had happened?

Evidence from elsewhere in the Americas and abroad suggests the answer— epidemic diseases, striking long-isolated populations with no natural immunities. Smallpox, measles, even the common cold, were fatal. A few 18th-century accounts describe stricken Indian villages where 80 to 90 percent of the people died within a few days. A tragedy of this order may well have reduced brave Quigualtam to the lesser order of the Natchez.

Yet despite their shrunken numbers and modest new capital, the Natchez impressed the French. Indeed, today there is more documentary information about the

Riches from the last capital of the Natchez, the Fatherland site: This brass tripod pot came to light in the grave of a personage described by archeologist Robert S. Neitzel as "easily the most important individual buried in the temple mound." He thinks this must have been the sacred ruler known as the Great Sun. The Natchez acquired the pot, and the glass beads below, from French traders. A less lavish burial in the same mound contained the necklace.

Natchez than for all other tribes in the region combined.

Cuisine and crops are reported in more detail than methods of hunting. We learn that meats and fish are invariably boiled or roasted, and never served rare. Varieties and colors of maize are named, their properties described. A cold cornmeal porridge seemed so delicious to one settler that he published the recipe for use in France!

Feasts take place at every new moon. The most joyous salutes the renewal of the year, reckoned for March, the Month of Deer. A drama of battle re-enacts an ancient rescue of a Great Sun from the surprise attack of enemies; the living Sun leads a silent rite at the temple, and then appears in full regalia to receive the gifts of his people.

At the harvest feast, the most solemn of all, the Great Sun is carried by senior warriors in a litter of state, draped with painted deerskins and garlanded with red and white flowers. At the ceremonial ground he rides a solemn circuit to salute the stores of grain. After a ritual rekindling of sacred fire in the temple, he distributes grain to the women of the people. A concert of song and a night of dancing by torchlight follow the feast; the next day brings a strenuous game, played with a ball of deerskin stuffed with Spanish moss, between a team for the great war chief and another for the Great Sun.

Recounted at length, these ceremonies let us imagine the year's round of life at the silent sites: Cahokia or Emerald or Moundville. And the funeral of the great war chief of the Natchez, the Tattooed Serpent—watched and described by his friend Antoine Le Page du Pratz—lets us appraise the treasures and sacrifices of the nameless grandees of Cahokia.

When the Tattooed Serpent died, ten victims were slain in his honor; and a noblewoman whom the French called La Glorieuse chose to offer her own life out of friendship, "to join him in the country of the spirits." His favorite wife calmly explained to the French that they should not grieve, they would be friends hereafter. There "nothing is wanting to live better than in this country. Men do not make war there any more, because they make only one nation."

Often, as we might expect, the French accounts are contradictory. For example, André Penicaut describes the Great Sun's house as "very large; it can hold as many as 4,000 persons." Others, including the usually reliable du Pratz, call the house about 30 feet square; and the archeology supports them.

With all of their flaws, these accounts reveal the confrontation of alien worlds. No one expressed it better than the Tattooed Serpent.

He was brother to the Great Sun, and like him lived on the summit of a mound in the grand village. He was, almost certainly, a direct descendant of that haughty chief who had challenged de Soto. The sympathetic du Pratz wrote down his friend's anguished questions:

"Why did the French come into our country? We did not go to seek them: they asked for land of us because their country was too little.... We told them they might take land where they pleased, there was enough for them and for us;

that it was good the same sun should enlighten us both, and that we would walk as friends in the same path; and that we would give them our provisions, assist them to build, and to labor in the fields. We have done so: is not this true? What occasion then had we for Frenchmen? Before they came, did we not live better than we do, seeing we deprive ourselves of a part of our corn, our game, and fish, to give a part to them? In what respect, then, had we occasion for them? Was it for their guns? The bows and arrows which we used were sufficient to make us live well. Was it for their white, blue and red blankets? We can do well enough with buffalo skins which are warmer; our women wrought feather blankets for the winter, and mulberry mantles for the summer; which indeed were not so beautiful; but our women were more laborious and less vain than they are now. In fine, before the arrival of the French, we lived like men who can be satisfied with what they have; whereas at this day we are like slaves, who are not suffered to do as they please."

On the morning of November 29, 1729, the much-tried Natchez attacked the settlements near the grand village and killed hundreds of men, women, and children. A mere handful escaped.

The Natchez, themselves, were attacked and destroyed by French expeditions in the following years.

In this revenge, the French had native allies, the Tunica, the heirs of Quizquiz. They had moved downriver since de Soto's time and, slipping past their old enemies the Natchez, had settled on the

(Continued on page 98)

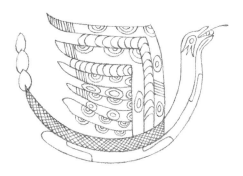

Symbols of the enigmatic Southern Cult suggest religious links with Mesoamerica to some archeologists. These examples occur on incised pottery from Moundville, Alabama. Hand-and-eye and skull motifs from a funerary urn may pertain to sun worship as well as to death. The feathered serpent might imply the Toltec god Quetzalcoatl and the Maya Kukulkan. The distinctive double-bird design, from a water bottle, apparently shows an ivory-billed woodpecker.

COTTON COULSON (BELOW AND OPPOSITE); HILLEL BURGER, THE PEABODY MUSEUM, HARVARD

Shrine of the Southern Cult, Moundville rests in the silence of ages by Alabama's Black Warrior River. Nineteen mounds, from three to twenty-three feet high, roughly encircle two larger burial mounds (above). Limited excavations have already uncovered more than 500 graves with rich stores of death offerings, among them this limestone effigy pipe. Identified as a jaguar or an ocelot, it held tobacco on the animal's back; a reed at the rear formed the mouthpiece. At right, three of the mounds viewed across one of the shallow ponds.

Under an overcast sky, a boy flies his kite from the top of Mississippi's Emerald Mound, 12 miles north of Natchez. The domelike summit, where a temple stood, itself rests on a man-made platform covering more than seven acres; the overall height from present-day ground level equals seventy feet. Long quarried by amateur relic collectors, Emerald now yields no trace of European contact; but some of de Soto's men undoubtedly saw this heart

of the Quigualtam nation. Archeologists recovered this Spanish brass bell and a little turquoise bracelet — the only turquoise of prehistory found east of the Mississippi River — in a child's grave at Edwards Mound near the city of Clarksdale.

MAXIMUM WIDTH 5¼ INCHES

*Conch shell from the Gulf of Mexico serves artists of prehistory:
The fragment above, from a large shell cup, depicts a man in
a canoe. The earliest such portrayal known, it evokes the armada
that de Soto saw in 1541. Three other fragments from the same
cup survive—all from the plundered Spiro site in Oklahoma. The
medallion below also came from Spiro. The gorget at right, found
in Missouri, almost matches one from Spiro; the author believes
"they were done by the same artist or by two men in the same
workshop. Both show a man taking part in some ceremony that
includes the game called chunkey, which was played with a stone
disk. This figure, by the way, is wearing a conch-shell pendant."*

DIAMETER 4¼ INCHES

MAXIMUM WIDTH 6 INCHES

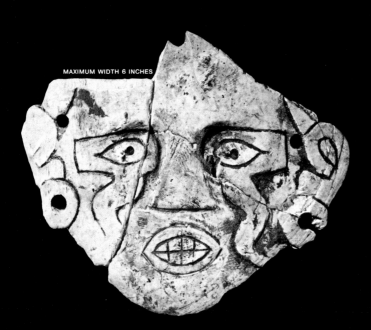

east bank near the mouth of the Red River.

Within the past decade a local treasure hunter, using the historic records as a guide, investigated a Louisiana hayfield with metal detectors. He made one of the great archeological finds of the century: the Tunica Treasure. Most of its artifacts are utilitarian items, of Indian and European manufacture. Yet in their exceptional quantity and variety they are a genuine treasure for the archeologist, who works most happily with the basic implements of human existence. Moreover, history supports the name. Father Charlevoix, missionary priest and historian of New France, visited the Tunica in 1721. He noted that the chief, one Cahura-Joligo, had "learned of us to hoard up money, and he is reckoned very rich. . . ."

I was able to excavate at the Tunica Treasure site in August 1972. The ghost of Cahura-Joligo, who was so enamored of white man's things, seemed to linger over the hayfield as we unlimbered our sophisticated instruments. Our magnetometer and other electronic gear identified the foundations, middens, and graves of a Tunica village. French maps indicated the period of settlement, about 1731 to 1764, and thus the artifacts we found became an unusually valuable set of references. Unbroken ceramics of the 18th-century Tunica can now be related to our potsherd chronology, our records of their ambitious journeys in the past.

Only seven people of Tunica descent still live on the tribal lands in Louisiana. Their last chief, Joseph Alcide Pierite, died March 16, 1976. He was the last in an unbroken continuity of chieftainship

that extends back through history into the prehistoric mists.

Chief Joe, as everyone called him, was buried in the tribal cemetery with appropriate regalia, such as a peace pipe and an eagle feather beaded with turquoise—the turquoise itself an ironic link with the child of Quizquiz. And in accordance with a custom of mourning fires, recorded by an 18th-century missionary priest, an eternal light of memorial will be placed over his grave. For, as I was told by Anna Mae Juneau, Chief Joe's daughter: "The chief should never be in the dark, it's a tradition."

So are we a little less in the dark. Traditions, manuscripts, archeology—they all cast a little light on the past. No matter how bizarre an individual story may seem, how perplexing a single item, the pieces are coming together.

Our potsherd collections and a distinctive arrowpoint let us recognize the "Cahokia horizon" in the lower valley: a few decades of contact with envoys from the north, about A.D. 1200. Thereafter we see a change in the southern site plans to the Cahokia pattern, and a flowering of the local cultures.

In the 1400's we see people abandon great centers by the Mississippi for new sites in the interior. By the time of de Soto's passage we find evidence for a stirring and movement of peoples, the Tunica among them.

For the Tunica especially, the traditions and the archeology reinforce the manuscripts, supporting some stories, clarifying others. But it is only in the manuscripts that something of the human drama of

events—of the nobility as well as baseness of men—is preserved.

Thus in the conflict of cultures, it is recorded by Rodrigo Ranjel that de Soto's men snatched babes from mothers' arms and fed them to their Irish greyhounds, "very bold, savage dogs" kept lean for just such terrifying purpose. "Oh, wicked men!" mourns the narrator: "...do not lament the conquered Indians less than their Christian conquerors or slayers of themselves, as well as others...."

Two hundred years later, in the self-styled Age of Reason, Le Page du Pratz set down his own well-considered observation: "When the Indians are treated insolently or oppressively, they have no less sensibility of injuries than others. If those who have occasion to live among them, will but have sentiments of humanity, they will in them meet with men."

*Dust turns to sunset gold near Hawikuh,
site of a Zuñi pueblo where the first Spanish
explorers sought treasure in vain. Francisco
Vásquez de Coronado in 1540 expected to find
it one of the fabled "Seven Cities of Cibola."
He found instead a proud, thriving village of
farmers who had no precious metals but
worked turquoise into beads. Rejecting many
novelties introduced by the Spaniards, the
Zuñi did accept sheep and learn the herder's
skills. Below, "two grand, solitary buttes of
rocks," described in Cushing's journals, rise
behind a present-day herder. In 1672
Apache horsemen attacked Hawikuh and
burned its Roman Catholic mission; the
Zuñi abandoned the site. Today a trading
post honors the name. The Zuñi only began
making metal jewelry in the 1830's; now
they derive most of their income from
silversmithing. Today Lyidianita Lasiloo
(at right, below) makes beadwork jewelry in
her home at Zuñi, for the tribal shops.*

On Tówayálane, or Corn Mountain,
the Zuñi took refuge from floods — as
told in myth — and from human foes
as recorded in history. Above, a small
half-ruined pueblo from the 1800's;
below, details of recent restorations —
adobe walls of the mission church at
Zuñi; a cross that separates graves
of men from those of women there.

O LORD
GRANT UNTO THEM
ETERNAL REST

BETWEEN TWO WORLDS:

WE DID NOT EXPECT to pluck gold bars from the clear waters of Bermuda. We even hoped the artifacts we found on our 17th-century shipwreck would have no monetary value—adventurers would not slip in for a fast haul that would ruin our archeological site.

In 1965, Edward (Teddy) Tucker had found the wreck that we would turn into an underwater classroom in 1972. He explored the site a couple of times with his friend Mendel Peterson, then director, Underwater Exploration Project, for the Smithsonian Institution. They picked up a coral-encrusted pewter container and nicknamed the ship "The Tankard."

Most people who know Teddy describe him as the underwater salvor who found the fabulous gold and emerald cross on a Spanish wreck. We who've worked with him know him as a scholar-diver with a remarkable ability to spot underwater objects that nobody else notices. I've heard him tell several times, in the British-tinged accent of Bermudians, what caught his eye about "The Tankard."

"I was cruising my boat along very slowly and looking at the sea floor through 30 feet of clear water. There were the usual dark-green patches of swaying sea grass on the white sand. I was some five miles off the northwest coast of the island, in sight of Somerset on Mangrove Bay.

"The area was full of coral reefs, some less than six feet below the surface. A dangerous spot for ships.

"I've always got my mind on seeing shapes that don't look entirely natural. I saw a pile of stones that were not natural to Bermuda's seabed. I stopped my boat.

The surface was like glass, and the late-afternoon sun was strong. I noticed a rectangular shadow across a patch of sand. Then I saw it was cast by a stump of timber. I knew right away the rocks were ballast and below them probably lay a wreck."

When Teddy and Mendel swam on the site, they agreed that some of the rocks were large nodules of flint. They suspected that the ship was probably wrecked before the 1680's, on the assumption that by then flintlock guns were making the stone too valuable for mere ballast. Such stone came from England or Normandy or Scandinavia, but that meant nothing— ships dumped ballast, or took it on, at need. Mendel and Teddy marked the site as worth attention someday.

Seven years later, 25 diving enthusiasts signed up for a three-week season of shipwreck archeology directed by Mendel and sponsored by Educational Expeditions International (EEI). Other instructors were Teddy, photographer Peter Stackpole, and two of us from the Smithsonian staff —conservator Joseph M. Young and myself as artist and illustrator.

With paying students we could study and record our ship right down to the keel.

We had worked other wrecks at the tolerance of treasure divers. Eager to find gold and silver, fretting about the daily cost of men and machinery, they had skimpy patience with the archeologist's methods. We wanted to fan sand away by the spoonful or airlift it gently for fear of damaging fragile artifacts; the salvors blew away a ton of sand within minutes with deflectors and compressed air, or even resorted to explosives.

THE FORTUNES OF THE SEA

Now we had our own site and eager, well-equipped workers. Among them were a Florida insurance agent and his wife, a surgeon from Connecticut, a physicist from Massachusetts, a Texas lawyer. In age, they ranged from teenagers to a pair of newlyweds in their 60's.

On Teddy's dive boat *Brigadier,* he outlined procedure. A "rock team" would clear away ballast; an "air gun team" would vacuum off sand; Peter Stackpole and I would record wreck structure and artifacts. Mendel told the artifact collectors to watch for bits of pottery, glass, leather, metal—"the slightest thing. Handle all objects lightly. Pick up every scrap and fragment you see. One of them might be a big clue to the ship's identity or the story of her loss."

The rock crews alternated 20-minute stints. They worked by what I've heard old merchant seamen call "Norwegian steam." That's biceps. The rest of us could make a tank of air last 40 minutes.

My first job was to hammer numbered iron spikes into the ship's timbers as they were cleared. This was the basis for an ingenious special grid of Mendel's that would govern the final drawing of the wreck. Our completed six-foot-long picture of the ship is a composite of hundreds of small sketches of individual timbers, keyed to the numbered spikes.

On our first day's dive I started drawing. For company I had several students and a swarm of inquisitive little fish. Sergeant majors are about finger-length; they arrived in squadrons and nipped at

A Wreck Found off Bermuda Yields Clues to the Ships of Settlement

By PETER COPELAND

CORAL-ENCRUSTED PEWTER VESSEL, POSSIBLY A TANKARD OR A MEASURE, FROM A 17TH-CENTURY SHIPWRECK. 6 1/2 INCHES HIGH.

Circling past coral heads, salvors from Bermuda row toward the crippled "Tankard," a merchant ship hung on a reef. Islanders hurry to strip her of cargo, masts, and rigging

before she sinks. Plans (background) from 1700 suggest her construction, but underwater excavation of the wreck in the 1970's brought new certainty to the history of shipbuilding.

Found among "Tankard" artifacts on the sea floor,
this brass spoon impresses experts as a product of
19th-century manufacture — much too late to belong

my pencil, my rope belt, and the back of my neck, as annoying as mosquitoes.

Some of my pupils were surprised to find that ordinary pencils work very well underwater on a matte surface of white acrylic plastic, and so do erasers.

Ashore in the evenings after a seven-hour day, we still had to copy our drawings. We simply laid tracing paper over the plastic boards, redrew our sketches, and inked them. Then we scrubbed off the boards for the next day's work. We also sketched all the specimens.

I'm often asked, "Why sketch and photograph the same things?" There are several reasons. If the light is poor — because of cloudy skies or deep water or turbid water — photographs will be poor. Even in good light, photographs don't show some details of complicated ship construction; drawings do — for example, the method of scarfing several timbers together. Photographs and sketches made from the same spot and studied side by side can bring the clear understanding that either alone might not.

Sketches are also insurance. I remember sketching a wooden jar top from a Spanish galleon wrecked off the Florida Keys, copying the handwritten name "D Juane de Ima." It was photographed at the same time. Next morning the writing had faded to invisibility, and it was illegible in the photograph, but my sketch had captured the letters as they appeared in those first moments out of the sea.

A similar example was a boot heel Teddy found during the first week on "The Tankard" wreck. Its three-inch height indicated it had probably been worn by a man of considerable wealth. Though handled gently, it fell apart very quickly once it had dried out. A photograph showed it as a globby gray-black mass — exactly how it looked as it came out of the water. My drawing showed just how it was made of leather held together by wooden pegs.

After three weeks of hard work on "The Tankard," our crew had removed about three layers of rock and sand from the stern section. In the bow, we'd done much less. But we knew she was all in one piece and mostly upright, a square-rigged, three-masted ship some 130 feet long, probably of 400 tons.

Early in the game, Teddy had told us which end was stern and which was bow. That came from his ability to recognize disturbances in the natural shapes of coral formations. One of the coral heads by the wreck had been broken in the past, he noticed; when he cut into the scar, he found traces of iron. Deeper in, he retrieved an iron gudgeon, or socket for the pintle of the rudder.

"The ship's stern hit there," Teddy said, "and probably tore a hole so big that she filled up quickly."

As for her artifacts, we'd noticed during the first days how firewood was mixed with the rocks. All the redware and majolica, porcelain and Venetian glass, were tiny bits. Mendel told us not to bother with recording the location of anything. "It would be meaningless," he said. "It's clear the ship had rolled violently, throwing everything back and forth and mixing it thoroughly."

From one rosary bead, a barely identi-

DRAWINGS BY PETER COPELAND

fiable Spanish coin, and the pottery, we judged that the ship was Spanish.

My own interest in costume let me contribute one small clue: a brass buckle, one and three-eighths inches by one and one-sixteenth. After 1660 buckles for shoes, and later for the knee straps of breeches, came into fashion for gentlemen.

At the moment I was more interested in a small leather shoe sole. It was round, tapering sharply toward the heel. A woman's shoe, I thought.

I drew it carefully; there was no way to preserve it. When I got back to Washington, D.C., I took the sketch to my friend Ernest Peterkin. For years his hobby has been research in shoemaking; he even makes his own shoes. He studied my drawing and finally said, "It seems to be from a shoe of the early 1500's, somewhat like those worn by the peasants in Pieter Bruegel's paintings. By its size, it's probably a boy's."

That date was more than a century too early for the buckle; but I had done a book on working people's clothes in past eras. I knew that such garments changed little from one century to another. My guess is that a cabin boy about ten years old wore that shoe—and that it was made as the shoemaker's family near his home had made shoes for generations.

I felt myself identifying with that boy. I went to sea myself when I was 16, and spent the 1940's and '50's on merchant ships. I've been fascinated all my life with the story of early seamen—the way they dressed, the living conditions they endured, the work they had to do, the length of their voyages. Few of them wrote their memoirs. But I can imagine a biography of a ship's boy to go with my sketch of that shoe sole. It would include an episode about an odd little stub-stemmed pipe that we found in the wreck. A boy might have carried such a piece in his pocket, a memento of his voyage to the New World.

When the last student had gone and Teddy and I were putting away the season's artifacts, he remarked, "It's a very peculiar collection. We've found two cannon balls and no cannon. We haven't found a single item from the rigging—blocks, deadeyes, sheaves, or anything like that."

(Deadeyes are roundish pieces of wood, fitted in pairs on each of the shrouds that support the mast. Sheaves are little wooden wheels that fit inside the blocks for ropes to ride on; sailing ships had scores of blocks.)

We talked this over a long time, and Teddy began to reconstruct the story of the wreck: "About a thousand feet to seaward of the wreck site, I found a place in the reef where large chunks of coral were broken off long ago. Perhaps 'The Tankard' broke them off. If she hit the reef in a storm, her crew would have had time to cut away her masts and rigging, and throw any cannon she had overboard. That might have kept her afloat until she struck that coral head."

It sounded very probable—until one bright day the following August. Our second group of EEI volunteers had begun clearing toward the bow. They unearthed a small hanging knee, or right-angle wooden brace, and a large piece of frame timber, which I duly sketched. On *Brigadier's* deck hours later, Teddy asked,

"Did you see those two timbers we dug out this morning?" I said, "Yep."

"Did you see the V notches cut into the wood?" "Yep." "Know what they are, don't you?" "Nope."

"Ax marks. *Salvors'* ax marks." I felt as if I'd swallowed a handful of deadeyes.

"Salvors hacked into the wood to remove the iron pins," Teddy went on. "That means 'The Tankard' was hung up on the coral quite a while. They had time to go through her with a fine-tooth comb. Lord knows how they missed that piece of pewter we found."

Before long, Teddy had found hacked timbers under the turn of the bilge on the port side. They told him that the ship lay on her starboard side as she hung on the coral head; otherwise, those timbers would have been underwater where salvors couldn't get at them. He thought the ship was stuck to the coral for weeks. Finally a battering storm would have knocked her loose and sent her sliding bow first into the sandy trench where he had found her.

Teddy had known that wreck salvage figured in Bermuda's economy in early years, but he'd never come across an example before. From his own diving experience, he reasoned that "The Tankard" came to grief in winter—because she wasn't burned.

In warm, calm, bright weather, wrecks were stripped of goods and then burned. Iron items fell to the bottom; divers, holding their breath, picked them out of the sand. But under dark skies, bolts and nails and hinges might not be visible; wind-tossed seas would quickly bury such small

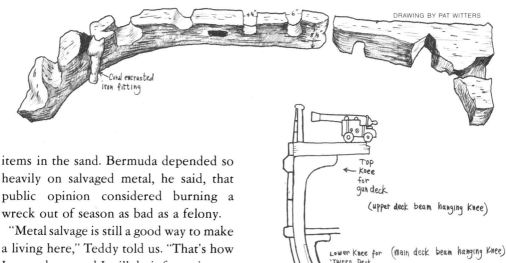

Coral encrusted iron fitting

Top Knee for gun deck

(upper deck beam hanging knee)

Lower Knee for 'Tween Deck

(main deck beam hanging knee)

Broken off at turn of BILGE

Keel

items in the sand. Bermuda depended so heavily on salvaged metal, he said, that public opinion considered burning a wreck out of season as bad as a felony.

"Metal salvage is still a good way to make a living here," Teddy told us. "That's how I started out, and I still do it from time to time — I take brass and copper and lead from wrecks later than 1860."

Now we felt sure "The Tankard's" salvors would have taken her masts, for use in other vessels. They took deck planking, for building houses. The cargo they could convert to cash. We knew from the small pieces we'd found that it included mahogany, other woods used for dye and inlay, tobacco, West Indian cowhides, and Chinese porcelain.

That porcelain would have brought a tidy profit if any had survived unbroken. It came from China by way of Manila in the Philippines, where Spanish ships picked it up and brought it to Acapulco, Mexico. Porcelain was prized by Europeans then and later as a status symbol.

On "The Tankard" site we found fragments of 18 patterns. Some were of the Wan-li period, named for the emperor who died in 1619. According to John A. Pope of the Freer Gallery of Art, an outstanding authority on ceramics of the Far East, other patterns would belong to the later 17th century. Some of this porcelain might have been the property of wealthy passengers who brought it along for their own use, but some was surely cargo.

Bermuda's salvage records would tell us the cargo, the name of the ship, and perhaps the names of survivors — or so we imagined. But these documents are often

Ax-scarred timber from the interior port frame bears deep cuts made by salvors who removed iron fittings; the diagram portrays it undamaged, from top knee to broken end at the turn of the bilge. Later finds indicated a flatter bottom. Overleaf: In an on-site underwater classroom, two students examine details of construction amidships. Teddy Tucker saws a section out of the oak keelson to compare it with the pine ribs and assess the soundness of the shipwright's work in the 1600's. "Shipbuilding was done out of the men's heads," he says; "they often cut their timbers without measuring them."

Author Peter Copeland sketches scattered ballast and exposed timbers of the starboard side near the stern — one of many detailed views that supplement the artist's report below. There, numbered iron spikes outline the partly excavated "Tankard" in a trench between two reefs and record the progress of the work in 1972. His underwater drawings, more than a hundred in all, included every board, joint, and pin. From these, from a day-to-day photographic documentation, and from historic evidence, experts can now reconstruct with confidence the hull structure of a large 17th-century cargo vessel.

*Probing the maritime past of the New World,
archeologist and historian Mendel Peterson goes
twenty feet down in Bahama waters to examine*

vague; fire and hurricanes have destroyed some of them. We would have to go on calling her "The Tankard."

Teddy estimated that she would have had a crew of 50 at most. A hundred passengers would have crowded her; and if a wealthy merchant or powerful official was on board — as we surmised from the fragments of valuables like Venetian glass — he would have paid well for comfortable space. (Incidentally, we never found even so much as a hint that any women were aboard "The Tankard.")

All this while, Teddy and I were having second thoughts about the future of our excavation on a salvaged wreck. As the season closed, we sat one evening under the poinciana trees on Teddy's lawn and came to a decision.

"We're ten feet down in the hull, with only five more to go," he pointed out. "We've sampled the keelson and know it's all there. This is the first 17th-century vessel I've seen with so much of her hull intact. She's the type of vessel that the early American colonists came in. Replicas have been built of ships like the *Mayflower*, or the *Susan Constant* at Jamestown, but some of their construction details had to be pure conjecture."

He brought out a couple of 17th-century engravings that purported to show midsection details and profiles. "Very few of these exist," he said, "and most of them show warships. And how accurate were the artists? They contradict each other, and the written descriptions as well.

"As far as I know," Teddy went on, "no museum anywhere preserves a whole specimen of a large cargo vessel from this period. There's the 1626 *Sparrow Hawk* at Plymouth, Massachusetts; but she's only 40 feet long, and a skeleton. Of course there's the 1628 *Vasa* in Stockholm, but she's a warship. Besides, she didn't survive her maiden voyage because of poor design." I began to feel the excitement of a new learning venture.

Besides, by this time we had grown rather fond of "The Tankard." We knew we must come back to her and, like salvors after cargo, strip her of information to her keel. The most interesting and telling details of her construction still lay under sand and rocks.

Students signing up for a two-week dig in August 1974 brought our diving crew to ten, plus Teddy, Peter Stackpole, and myself. We would work purely for history and archeology; and the Philadelphia Maritime Museum subsidized us handsomely. Its grant covered salary and expenses for Peter and me, and other costs as well.

Soon we had proof that "The Tankard" differed in construction from warships, which were almost invariably built with solid oak for strength. Her inner hull was finished with planks called ceiling. We pried them off with crowbars to examine the framing, and Teddy identified the wood as pine. Most other timbers were softwoods, spruce or pine; a few floor riders were fir, and so was the bruised and dented keel, with a strip of oak shoeing the bottom edge.

Only critical timbers were oak: the keelson, most of the floor riders, the outer planking of the hull, and all the knees. The keelson turned out to be several pieces of

remains of a 16th-century warship, a smaller vessel than "The Tankard."
Surviving portions show a sharp bow and stern, suggesting a light ship
built for speed—possibly, says Mr. Peterson, a pirate ship or privateer.

oak, scarfed together; we learned later that by 1600 Europe faced a "materials crisis" in shipbuilding, a scarcity of big oak trees. As a result, cargo ships were put together with the woods a builder could lay hands on.

My sketching pupils and I noticed many variations in construction. Finding bracing timbers fastened at certain points on the starboard side didn't mean we would find the same treatment on the port side. It was as if two sets of shipwrights had built her, each following his own ideas on how to strengthen her.

Craftsmanship varied as well. Most floor timbers, for example, were neatly finished on all four sides, but at least one still had bark on two sides. I remember the incredulity on the face of one of our divers when he saw that—he was a Navy commander.

But Teddy, who spent quite a bit of time studying the hull, was prepared to say that "The Tankard" came from a tradition of building ships for dangerous waters. She had an extra layer of sheathing from the turn of the bilge to just above load line, a useful protection in icy seas. That, along with the quantity of fir, spruce, and pine, suggested origin in a northern country, possibly in Scandinavia.

The center stretch of her bottom was as flat as a barge's—this turned our speculation to the Netherlands, where wide flat bottoms were more of a tradition.

We had no trouble reconciling this with all our evidence that "The Tankard" had sailed under Spanish colors. As early as 1588, when Spain sent her unlucky "Invincible Armada" against England, the

NATIONAL GEOGRAPHIC PHOTOGRAPHER OTIS IMBODEN

White glaze
Blue design
Thickness: 3/32"
Porcelain

DRAWINGS BY TIMOTHY D. HOLTSLAG

Side #1 Side #2
Thickness: 3/32"

Blue lines, wipe outs at firing;
blue glaze
Background
Porcelain

Mediterranean countries had little oak suitable for shipbuilding. By 1600 Spain was short of all woods. The Spanish were chartering or buying large ships from England, the Netherlands, Scandinavia, and the Hanseatic German builders for trade with the New World.

In the northern countries before 1700, and more often thereafter, many ships were built by plans in the head of the individual shipwright. "The Tankard's" quirks of construction may be surprising today, but not beyond explaining.

Drawings and plan views of 17th-century vessels are rare. But just recently I saw a new facsimile edition of a Dutch book from 1700, *Architectura Navalis et Regimen Nauticum,* a treatise on shipbuilding by one Nicolaes Witsen. Not only did its engravings resemble the structure of "The Tankard" more than any other illustrations I've seen, they also straightened us out on one point. We had identified certain timbers as reinforcements. Witsen's plates show these as sections of interior frame timbers. For lack of single timbers of adequate size and curved shape, several pieces or "futtocks" are overlapped and fastened together—a second-best method, perhaps, but a thoroughly practical one.

Moreover, Teddy reasoned, "The Tankard" had lasted thirty years or so. "She has lead patches on her hull, always a sign of age and use. And she's been caulked at least four times. I could see fragments of four types of caulking materials. If a wooden ship wasn't caulked all over every few years, she was bound for trouble. Incidentally, there're no barnacles on her hull, which means she'd just been ca-

reened. I'd guess it was done in the West Indies before she headed home—some of her ballast rocks have corals that don't grow north of Hispaniola."

So we put together more of the life history of our wreck. All the while, I was furiously measuring timbers and drawing sketches of every board, joint, and pin, from sheathing to floor timbers. Peter Stackpole took hundreds of color photographs. We both knew our record would be invaluable. Every night I redrew my sketches to scale, fitting them into the overall diagram. Mendel says they're the most complete, detailed drawings he knows of the lower hull structure of a 17th-century merchant ship drawn from existing archeological material.

I've had many rewards from our three summers of work on "The Tankard." The biggest has been learning about old ships, artifacts, and wreck excavation from Teddy and Mendel. Recently it has led to another job with Mendel, doing the work I've come to love: diving and sketching a still-nameless man-of-war on the Little Bahama Bank.

And most of us who worked "The Tankard" took away prized memories of personal contacts with those unfortunate people of another century. We can hope they survived; we have no proof they didn't. The only bones we ever found were those of fish and domestic animals, from the ship's stores of salted food.

Once I was one of the poor devils aboard a ship that struck a reef. You can't imagine beforehand the terrifying jolt, or the shock of watching from a lifeboat as your ship is swallowed up.

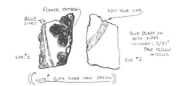

Even in disaster, 17th-century protocol should have ruled. The rich and important should have had a seat in the officers' boat. Crewmen were expendable—no lifeboat for them. But then, as Mendel says, the boat probably went to the man with the biggest pistol.

Mendel quotes an account by a survivor of a 1639 disaster, when two Spanish ships were hanging on the Bermuda reefs. The passengers were building rafts when they saw small boats approaching, "like herons in flight twisting and turning as they cut through the restless waves." The Bermudians salvaged everything they could budge.

The rescued Spaniards, in Mendel's words, were "boarded out in private homes at high rates. They were kept on the islands till the Bermudians fleeced them well." But they had survived.

Perhaps "The Tankard's" shell collector lived to pay high rates to an island family—we found an assortment of rare shells from the Caribbean, South American, and South Pacific waters.

One of Teddy's favorite memories concerns the moment he glimpsed in the sand a portrait of a Spanish gentleman, painted on majolica. "For a second," he recalls, "I felt our eyes had met."

One of mine concerns a stone axhead four inches long, grooved for lashing to a cleft-stick handle. I imagined when I first saw it that a passenger was taking it home to his son. Probably the father thought his boy would be thrilled to own a tool made by a real Indian of New Spain. But of course it traveled no farther than Bermuda's murderous reefs.

Styles of Old and New Worlds appear on fragments of cups, plates, and bowls. Glazed colors and patterns identify two samples as Chinese porcelain, three as majolica made in Mexico. Given a symmetrical design—as on the majolica plate below—archeologists can restore the whole from a couple of pieces; and a bit of base or rim lets them project the shape of the rest, as this side view indicates.

TOP VIEW

SIDE VIEW

DRAWINGS BY STEVEN MAKOVENYI

Veteran treasure diver Teddy Tucker muses over his finds—the pewter vessel that may have measured wine, fragments from "The Tankard," and less damaged pieces, such as an intact bottle, from another wreck of the period. "Tankard" artifacts conform to styles of the 17th century: a clay pipe, a brass buckle, majolica from Mexico, and Tucker's favorite—a haunting portrait on a majolica sherd. With such details, the ship's last crew, her archeological team, has prepared a full account of a workaday merchantman: an invaluable record for historians of the sea.

OUTPOSTS AND CAPITALS:

"RAISE YOUR MUSKETS! Try your match! Present!" A dozen men were facing me only a few feet away, all sighting down their gun barrels. "Give fire!" Instinctively I ducked as the guns went off. "Shoulder your muskets!" shouted the captain, and I remembered that he was the stand-in for Miles Standish of Plymouth, Massachusetts, in 1621.

"About face! March!" And the Pilgrim army tramped toward the meeting house.

I had just been reading the words "we exercised our arms" in the only Pilgrim account of this occasion—the one I had known since childhood as Thanksgiving. Edward Winslow had written of it. The staff researchers at re-created Plimoth Plantation had studied the findings of historical archeologists, and now they were putting the results on display. They had concluded that Winslow was describing not the Thanksgiving of American tradition but the traditional Harvest Home festival of English farmers.

Various surprises at the re-enactment had shaken me: the date, in early October; the sports; the dancing; the songs. And the gun drill had startled me as it had the 17th-century Indians.

I noticed a Pilgrim woman wearing a bodice of black wool homespun and an ankle-length skirt as red as the pokeberries in the woods beyond the palisade. She was cooking a bucket of clams at a tripod over an open fire.

"Where's the turkey?" I asked. "I see Winslow doesn't mention turkey."

The cook faces hundreds of thousands of visitors from May through October. She laughed and said, "Oh, we're pretty sure the Pilgrims had turkey at their festival. Governor William Bradford didn't write about this event—maybe he disapproved of it—but he did give details on the hunting in those weeks. He said the men brought home many ducks, geese, and wild turkeys. Just think of feeding 50 Pilgrims and 90 Indians for nearly a week! They needed dozens of fowl every day.

"You should talk with Dr. Deetz, our archeologist," she went on; "he's just down Leyden Street over there."

Leyden—originally "the street" as distinguished from "the highway"—is the longer of two streets in "new" Plimoth, begun in 1958 on a slope by the sea two miles from the town on the 1620 site. Laughing youngsters in costume and garlands were skipping in line down its rain-gullied surface, singing 17th-century songs. One stiff-shouldered woman screamed at the dancers, "Fie on you! Fie on you!"

I found James Deetz in Pilgrim dress, directing a crowd of volunteer actors. When he had sent them off to play colonists and Indians, he listened to my question: "What told you, Dr. Deetz, that Winslow was not describing a thanksgiving but a festival?"

"Well, I noticed the absence of the word 'thanks.' The Pilgrims had thanksgivings, sometimes several times a year, depending on the blessings sent by Heaven. These were days proclaimed when needed, to acknowledge God's favors. For example, the Pilgrims had a July thanksgiving in 1623 for a rain that broke a drought. They had long worship services then, with more fasting than feasting.

"They weren't opposed to feasting and

THE COLONIAL YEARS

sports as such, only on days of prayer—Winslow mentions 'recreations' in October 1621. With my friend Jay Anderson, a folklorist at Penn State, I looked up English customs of the period, and Harvest Home festival exactly fitted."

He told me about Henry VIII's edict that the harvest must be completed before farmers began their celebration. For a week nothing went on except feasts and "recreations"—sports, games, dancing.

Then how, I asked, did we get our notion of Thanksgiving? "I'd say it evolved in the Puritan towns of New England in something of the way English puddings evolved into American pies. By the Revolution, the Thanksgiving tradition of roast turkey, pumpkin pie, cranberry sauce, and prayer was fixed in New England. But the date wasn't; each town chose its own time."

A nationwide Thanksgiving Day was an innovation of President Abraham Lincoln's, I found out later. In giving the whole country the holiday of New England, he followed George Washington's choice of date—the last Thursday in November 1789 had been a "thanksgiving" for the adoption of the new Constitution.

Lincoln proclaimed "Thanksgiving" in 1863, largely at the insistence of New Englander Sarah J. Hale. She had been promoting the idea during 36 years as writer and editor of *Godey's Ladies Book*. Issued in October, the proclamation reminded fellow citizens everywhere of blessings enjoyed in spite of civil war, and urged them to pray fervently for the restoration of "peace, harmony, tranquillity, and Union."

Rediscovering Places of Settlement, "Lost" Incidents of Colonial Life

By TEE LOFTIN
National Geographic Staff

PORCELAIN FRAGMENT WITH GOVERNOR LORD DUNMORE'S
COAT OF ARMS, WILLIAMSBURG, VIRGINIA 1775.

Year after year, American Presidents renewed the Thanksgiving holiday. Year by year the New England menu and the Pilgrim myth fixed themselves in the national heart.

"Changing the nature of Thanksgiving today isn't the purpose of our re-enactment at Plimoth," Dr. Deetz told me. "We're only showing with historical accuracy the old English autumn festival that Edward Winslow referred to."

Why do all this re-creating, reconstructing of old villages and old ways? For one thing, Americans are intensely interested in seeing them. Almost year round, they crowd places like Plimoth Plantation, Old Sturbridge Village and Old Salem in Massachusetts, Williamsburg in Virginia, the Moravian Salem in North Carolina, and Old Town in San Diego, California.

Moreover, bringing our past to life, with real people re-enacting an old culture in an authentic setting, is the adrenalin of historical archeology.

"When you begin doing or making specific things instead of just talking about them," Dr. Deetz said, "you discover that you don't know much. You have to look for more clues to guide you. You have to search for answers in the earth, in records, inventories, literature, land titles, relics still in use, graveyard tombstones — and, as our Indian staff members tell us, in dreams and visions.

"At Plymouth, we find we must re-create not New England culture — that only began developing with the first settlers' children — but rural English culture of the early 1600's. The settlers transported it bodily to the New World. That culture was medieval, closer to 1492 in type than to 1776."

At the end of the chilly afternoon, while the ocean writhed and foamed at the edge of the village, Pilgrims and Indians stood hungrily around a rough wooden table. They had shared such chores as cleaning a yard-long codfish and preparing a pit and grill to roast sheep. Now they could feast, taking morsels of mutton with their fingers in the best manners of the early 1600's. They sat on the ground or on logs, sharing wooden bowls and leather mugs.

"It wasn't the age of a chair, a plate, a cup for each member of a family," Dr. Deetz remarked. "That brand-new concept of having sets of things, even matching sets, began to revolutionize their economy and culture about 1750."

When a drizzle thickened into rain, we retreated to a house. Fire blazed on a hearth nearly the width of the room. But the chimney was hearth-width to its top, and wind and rain made the fire sputter. We shivered. Dr. Deetz grimaced. "This is a case where we went ahead without knowing much. Now we admit that these houses are mostly wrong. The chimneys are very wrong. They should be wattle-and-daub, not stone. They should be smaller, and tapered at the top."

Only in 1973 did the Plimoth researchers find hard archeological evidence for the houses the Pilgrims built, and then only from a chance discovery. Insurance agent Orfeo Sgarzi retired, and bought a waterside lot some two miles along the bay from Plymouth. Workmen digging a foundation for his home turned up some pottery scraps — a signal to call Dr. Deetz.

But only y gndeans, and they had no trading comodities;

FROM BRADFORD'S MANUSCRIPT WRITTEN BETWEEN 1630 AND 1650, FOLIO 181, LIBRARY OF CONGRESS (ABOVE)

"The findings were early 17th-century," he told me, "and the excitement began."

Plymouth records are so extensive that it took a student two weeks to find that in 1627 the land had belonged to *Mayflower* passenger Isaac Allerton. A hearth and soil stains indicated that Master Allerton's farmhouse had an earth floor and a post frame—a squared tree trunk at each corner to hold up the roof and rafters.

Dr. Henry Glassie of the University of Pennsylvania, a specialist in vernacular architecture (or homemade buildings), had spent all the summer of 1974 directing the construction of the first small post-frame house at the Plantation. Another is now being built, and more houses will be constructed in the same fashion.

Plymouth, the second permanent English colony in America, has no monopoly on the search for the specific and on notable discoveries. Near Jamestown, Virginia, where the first permanent English colony took root, a retired banker and an archeologist have bumped into what may be the first evidence of one type of medieval dwelling found in America.

The banker, David A. Harrison, took a leisurely stroll in a soybean field by the James River one day in 1971. He had recently bought a plantation called Flowerdew Hundred, on the south shore about 20 miles upstream from Jamestown.

"As I was enjoying the view, I stumbled over something," Mr. Harrison told me. "It turned out to be clay roofing tile. I was at a place called Windmill Point, so I decided the tile had some connection with an old, old windmill."

(Continued on page 132)

COTTON COULSON

Writing his famous chronicle of the Pilgrims, Of Plimoth Plantation, *Governor William Bradford makes brief references to the Algonquian tribes of Massachusetts. But colonist Edward Winslow's accounts, and others, give rich detail today to Indians reviving their ancestors' customs and skills. Re-created Plimoth now includes an Indian summer camp, where Naomi Andrews picks ripe pokeberries, used with other natural ingredients for face paint. Pilgrims learned from their neighbors about native "pocan," or dye-yielding plants.*

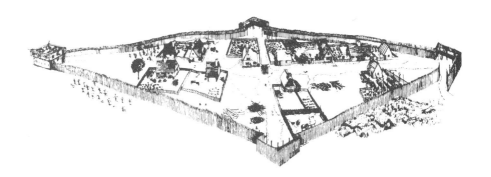

From morning garland-weaving to end-of-day chatter, women of re-created Plimoth Plantation prepare for the Harvest Home festival. Research reveals that Winslow's account of the Pilgrims' first celebration referred to a lighthearted English autumn event, not a grave "thanksgiving." A dig in 1973 supplied some corrections for houses (left) built in the 1950's and 1960's, says archeologist James Deetz. Newer cottages have walls and tapered chimneys of wattle and daub, tiny windows, thatch roofs. From a description by a Dutch visitor of 1627, and a diagram by Bradford, an artist drew the village plan above.

COTTON COULSON; ERIC ENGSTROM, PLIMOTH PLANTATION (ABOVE)

Last-minute housecleaning
and adjusting a sword belt
preoccupy "Pilgrims"
at Plimoth Plantation
on festival morn. Shortly
the militiaman will drill
and shoot; the maid—as
young as Priscilla Mullins
in 1621—will dance
garlanded with flowers; the
matron will cook fowl, fish,
meat pasties, and puddings.
From close-fitting white
coif to stout wool jacket of
handwoven cloth, costumes
reflect the thorough
research of historians.

They begane now to geather in ye small harvest they had

By autumn of 1621, says Bradford, the colonists "had all things in good plenty."
Winslow wrote that settlers rejoiced after the harvest with feasting and "recreations."
At a Plimoth re-enactment with 17th-century food, games, and manners, a boy rests
a moment with his mother while companions roll inside a barrel hoop. Eating pit-
roasted meat and drinking beer, Pilgrims and Indians share a few mugs and bowls.

He mentioned his find to archeologist Norman Barka of the College of William and Mary, and Dr. Barka came out to make a test dig on the river bank.

"About a foot beneath my soybeans," Mr. Harrison said, "he dug out pieces of 17th-century glass, clay pipes, and pottery. I found it pretty exciting. Those old bits and pieces led me deep into the historical archeology business."

He invested a considerable sum to establish Southside Historical Sites, Inc., a nonprofit foundation for archeological research in Virginia. Collaborating with the College of William and Mary, the foundation hired Dr. Barka as supervising archeologist; he and a group of students began work in 1972 at the Flowerdew site.

"I think we've found a unique American example of a medieval English 'cruck' house, the predecessor of today's A-frame," Dr. Barka told me. "At least, no one has a better explanation for the oddity we've uncovered. In a stone foundation, we have curious matching gaps in the walls and corners, some 10 and some 18 inches wide. I believe that the bases of four 'cruck' or A-shaped arches sat in those gaps and served as the house frame.

"It's a convenient way to put up corner posts and rafters as a unit, if you have curved tree trunks. But there's been no archeological evidence of a 'cruck house' in America until now—*if* now."

Some yards from that house, Dr. Barka's team found a well seven feet deep, a forge, and postholes indicating three dwellings. "This group was surrounded by a fence, according to the great number of postholes. At first we thought we had

a log palisade—documents refer to one. It could have accounted for Flowerdew's surviving the 1622 Indian attack when a third of Virginia's thousand settlers were killed. But the larger postholes were several feet apart. We had to conclude that the fence was the wattle-and-daub type. Perhaps one day we'll find postmolds from that strong palisade—we know it was stoutly defended."

The plantation, apparently named for its pioneer settler Stanley Flowerdew, had some 60 people in 1625, more than most settlements on the James. But owner succeeded owner; dwellings rotted and disappeared. The old site was forgotten—until David Harrison stumbled over a piece of tile.

Now it will begin a second life, for paying visitors. Mr. Harrison brought millwright Derek Ogden from England, with several tons of oak for him to turn into a working windmill.

"We're hoping to reconstruct buildings at the settlement center, some of the shoreline palisade, and possibly a wharf," Dr. Barka said. "I'm pretty sure a few hours of underwater archeology would confirm that a long wharf ran out to the river channel. After storms, we find a concentration of artifacts on the beach—pottery, iron, tools, even gun fragments."

Downriver at Jamestown, archeologist Paul Hudson was also wishing for a few hours of underwater research. As we stood near the statue of John Smith, Paul pointed over the water to the probable site of the first fort. "In 1607, out there was a point of land, and ships in the channel could tie up to the trees. We're not sure

contract and a dig on the nearby site made possible a strict authenticity.
Structures planned for "the crossroads capital" will represent periods from
the 1630's, when Assemblies met in officials' parlors, until about 1700.

when the old fort disappeared, but it's not mentioned after 1625; and today the water is only knee deep over the old point.

"It recedes 50 to 75 feet about once a year," he went on, "when strong winds push and strong tides pull during storms. When that happens, I've walked out to where John Smith's fort may have been. I dug there, too. I never had time between tides to get beyond the 20th-century soft-drink bottles, but I feel certain that an underwater survey would turn up much 17th-century material."

Back in Washington, I consulted Mendel Peterson, retired head of underwater archeology at the Smithsonian. What did he think about an underwater survey at Jamestown?

"Where ships anchor to load and unload," he said, "there're bound to be things falling or being thrown into the water—wood, metal, ceramics. A covering of James River mud would preserve them. The chances are high, I think, that a magnetometer printout would indicate metal weapons or armor, anchors, that sort of thing. The river was probably the trash pit of the settlers as well as the sailors."

But today even a bargain-priced electronic survey would cost $10,000—too much for a strained budget.

I went on to Annapolis, Maryland, to look into an electronic probing of written history. In the State Hall of Records, historian Lois Green Carr gave me a step-by-step account of how she files many small facts in a computer memory.

She brought out a probate ledger containing lists of possessions of 17th-century Marylanders at the time they died.

COTTON COULSON

Demanding the right to vote like other taxpayers, Mistress Margaret Brent meets bemused resistance from fellow Marylanders in 1648. The governor denied her petition. The artist has created faces; but documents, and remains of a house called "St. John's" in St. Mary's

City, enabled archeologists to draw plans (above) of the parlor where this early appeal
for women's rights took place. "We excavated the very room," says archeologist Garry Stone.
"Mistress Brent stood on a plank floor fastened to the joists with 570 handwrought nails."

In quill-and-ink handwriting, the inventories cited everything except land — from empty bottles to black slaves.

Then Dr. Carr showed me how the names and inventory items look after she has sorted them into categories and assigned each a code number. "With the bits of information stored as numbers on tapes," she said, "the computer can re-sort and rearrange the facts according to any scheme we devise.

"By themselves, inventory items and individual names are mere statistics — lifeless artifacts like a boxful of pipe stems or potsherds. Relating them to other types of information, we can have a broader picture in a few seconds. Like this." She held up a line graph and a table of data.

"The graph's peaks and valleys chart the mean of estate wealth year by year; the table shows which people owned what proportion of the wealth.

"We're connecting this study to names in our file of careers — we've drawn together a biographical census of 17th-century Marylanders — so we can see the quality of material life in each household.

"We're locating those households geographically, too," Dr. Carr continued. "But we're doing it by hand. From boundary descriptions we chart the shapes of the farms, allowing for lost landmarks. Then we can place them just about where they belong on area maps."

I saw an example of these land-record graphics on the southwest shore of the Chesapeake near the Potomac River's entrance into the bay. This was at the site of St. Mary's City, the village that Governor Leonard Calvert founded in 1634 and made Maryland's capital for 60 years. Archeologist Garry Stone pointed out the route of Aldermanbury Street in 1670.

"As you see, this is just open farmland now," he said. "The location of street and houses has long been lost. Lois found all the lot surveys and drew up charts from the descriptions. When she had located the row of lots, she knew the street went past it."

Here state-supported archeologists are uncovering house foundations; and the state has sponsored reconstruction of the 1676 capitol. (The colonists themselves called this building their statehouse, meaning simply a place for the business of government, and the name has been kept.) By 1984 a museum-village is to summarize three centuries of life at St. Mary's.

"This was the third English capital in America," said Garry, "and the site is intact — not destroyed by river erosion like Jamestown or covered by modern construction like Plymouth. In the early 1660's the 'capitol' was the governor's house or his secretary's, and the 'capital' was just their farms and outbuildings. The population hadn't gone over a hundred." But thousands of Marylanders passed through every year, to do business at the seat of government.

That wealthy and spirited woman Mistress Margaret Brent, for example, came to argue cases at law. She also argued in 1648 that if she served as attorney for the Lord Proprietor — which she did, by court order — she should have a seat in the colony's Assembly. She wanted a "vote in the howse for herselfe and voyce allso." The governor denied this. But the assembly-

*a colonist in 1585 on Roanoke Island, then part of Virginia's ill-defined expanse.
Meager phrases written by Jamestown settlers, and studies of English architecture,
helped in reconstructing the fort's dwellings. Barrel hoops, awaiting use, lean
against a daub wall where wattles, or sticks, show through chinks in the clay.*

men informed Lord Baltimore that his affairs were "better for the Collonys safety ... in her hands than in any mans else in the whole Province...."

Both visitors and residents would leave traces of their stay, Garry remarked: "We expect that ten years of excavating within the 1,500 acres of townlands will unearth more than a million artifacts. To keep track of them, and to make rapid research use of them the way Lois Carr does with documentary facts, we'll need computer help too."

Of course that's expensive, he said; but so is rummaging through card files or cartons for, say, a full count of butterfly hinges from a hundred houses, and potsherds can be even more of a problem for record keepers.

Pottery, records, and good luck combined to produce a remarkable discovery at Yorktown, Virginia. Ivor Noël Hume, director of archeology for the Colonial Williamsburg Foundation, had identified fragments of stoneware found at Yorktown as saggers—ceramic containers that protect pottery placed in a kiln for firing. Saggers implied a kiln in or near Yorktown, and stoneware implied a potter skilled at his trade.

My friend Malcolm Watkins, a curator at the Smithsonian, searched the historical sources and found references to an unnamed "poor potter" at Yorktown. He tracked down a candidate for the role: one William Rogers, a brewer whose estate inventory included unusual quantities of pottery—such as 86 dozen mugs. Some of it was stoneware. "Rogers died a well-to-do man," Malcolm remarked. "He

COTTON COULSON

*Helmet, breastplate, and halberd emerged from
lumps of rust and bacterial scale uncovered on the
banks of the James River; dotted lines indicate*

owned two lots in Yorktown and I thought the kiln might be on them."

Back in 1959, the owner of those lots, truck driver Bill Childrey, had gotten a surprise one day when he looked into a water-main trench just dug in his backyard. It cut through a mass of unglazed redware, mostly broken pans.

"Of course in Yorktown you can hardly dig a hole big enough for a marigold without finding pieces of pottery," Bill told me recently, "but it seemed crazy to find so much, in such big pieces." Not thinking of history "any more than the man in the moon," he picked out half a dozen pieces and stacked them under a tree.

One of the trench diggers also took a piece. He used it as an ashtray at a gasoline station where he worked part-time. There, nearly a decade later, amateur archeologist Dean Bailey saw it and recognized a distinctive shape.

"I had studied the report published by Noël Hume and Watkins, and had poked around looking for the kiln myself," he told me. "I knew that was a milk pan with the 'Rogers' spout."

With his friend Norman Barka, Dean was soon examining the stack of pottery under Bill's tree. Bill showed them where the water line ran.

"We found a waster pit," Dr. Barka told me, "hundreds of cracked or misshaped or poorly glazed pieces. I knew the kiln was in wheelbarrow distance—but in which direction? We spot-tested for months, found nothing. Then I went off to England for the summer of 1970."

In the drawl of rural Tidewater Virginia, Bill Childrey picked up the story. "One day that summer, I cleaned out my garage. We'd used it for a workshop and I swept it real clean of sawdust and shavings. In the dirt floor, I saw pieces of brick sticking out, so I dug up a few. I had the lost kiln on my mind and decided to do a spot test with a piece of water pipe. I hammered the end into the ground. A few inches down, it hit something.

"When I pulled the pipe out, I could see flakes of green glaze in the soil sample it had collected. I knew from being around the spot-testing that they meant saltglaze for stoneware. Well, I tell you I got pretty excited, and so did Mrs. Barka when I telephoned her.

"A bunch of students with trowels came out next morning. Before dark, they'd scraped six inches of dirt off half the floor, and found the top of the kiln!"

"The whole pottery complex is here," Dr. Barka told me happily when I visited the site in the fall of 1975. "It's the most complete early 18th-century kiln and factory found in North America, the best preserved of its kind in the world. And the National Park Service is sponsoring our work on it now."

He blessed the luck that saved it from destruction during 250 years. No scavengers took the bricks; Revolutionary and Civil War earthworks skirted them; garage foundations just missed the underground structure; a proposed concrete floor for the garage was never poured.

And Bill? "Finding the kiln has done magical things for me. I never had much. But I sold my house and lots for a good price to the Park Service. Now I've got a new house, a car and truck, and I sure

the halberd's wooden shaft, long since rotted away. Chemicals applied to the carefully cleaned metal keep it from crumbling. Such equipment dates from about 1590 — evidence that settlers of 1607, and later, had to make do with discards.

enjoyed learning how to do archeology."

"Archeology is fun," Mr. Noël Hume agrees. A transplanted Englishman, he has supervised the excavations at Colonial Williamsburg since 1957. He laughed as he told me he sometimes felt like "a slayer of sacred cows" when artifacts disproved cherished assumptions.

For example, thousands of visitors have heard that George Washington, as a delegate to the House of Burgesses in the 1760's, stayed in a house on Duke of Gloucester Street. It had been a hostelry run by Mrs. Christiana Campbell until James Anderson, a blacksmith and armorer, bought the property in 1770.

The story was revised, said Mr. Noël Hume, "by a piece of pottery no bigger than a man's thumbnail. Recently we dug beneath a brick-lined drain believed to have been keyed into the house foundation." Under the drain was a creamware sherd, and 1769 is the first year when creamware is known to have been used in Virginia. "So Washington must have dined in a house destroyed before Mr. Anderson built that new one.

"But on the property we've dug up a collection of broken pottery, crab claws, bones of deer, cows, and poultry. Washington frequented Mrs. Campbell's dining room for a decade; he may have been served on that pottery and eaten the meat from some of those bones.

"One curious thing, though. For a tavern site, we found too few wine bottles. It is possible that Mrs. Campbell — said to be a dwarf and extremely rude — ran a lodging house, not a licensed tavern."

The restoration of a tavern owned by

In an artist's portrait for about 1625, Flowerdew Hundred plantation comes to life
by the James River, drawn from the archeological record of earth stains on the site. As
diagrammed (top), brown spots give shape and location of wooden posts for fences;

red, for buildings. Burned bits of clay bespoke wattle-and-daub chimneys; the lack of clay tile meant shingle or thatch roofs. Cobblestones mark a well. A 1625 census listed cattle and swine; 1622 records mention a windmill (extreme left), the first built in English America.

one Henry Wetherburn was a project Mr. Noël Hume found particularly exciting: the archeology of a standing building. "It's almost holy writ with many archeologists," he said, "that to be worthy of their attention a building must have been reduced to foundations and a scatter of debris." Here the archeology began at the roof and continued down to the cellars, in a complex deciphering of alterations and replasterings and repaintings.

Even animals had played a part — spaces between floor joists and behind laths contained nuts hidden by squirrels and chicken bones gnawed by rats.

While the archeological team was interpreting layers of ground outside the tavern, to establish dates for events in the life of the property, architects were applying archeological techniques inside. For instance, to determine the sequence of paint colors on the woodwork — a kind of vertical stratigraphy — they used solvents to remove the old paint one layer at a time.

But, says Mr. Noël Hume, "It is the pursuit of people that excites me; and it was the life and times of Henry Wetherburn that we were finding."

Some white fragments of English saltglaze stoneware provided clues to the patriotism of the times. They were decorated with slogans recalling Britain's alliance with Prussia against France during the Seven Years' War: "SUCCESS TO THE KING OF PRUSSIA AND HIS FORCES."

"In our experience," he explained, "these patriotic items tend to turn up most frequently on tavern sites, which I think has something to say about the social history of patriotism. Barroom patriotism is less self-conscious and inhibited than the cocktail-circuit variety."

The distribution of porcelain fragments at Williamsburg has something to add to the history of local sentiment during the Revolution. The last royal governor, Lord Dunmore, slipped out of his restive capital by night in June 1775, taking his wife and children; at Yorktown they boarded the ship *Fowey,* and it was from shipboard that Dunmore made his last efforts to exercise the authority of the Crown.

Among the many items Dunmore left in the Governor's Palace was porcelain from his dinner service, which bore his coat of arms. When the specialists for Colonial Williamsburg restored the Palace in the 1930's, they found two broken plates; but pieces of this ware have been discovered here and there around town. Patriots had helped themselves to souvenirs of the Palace that summer; evidently they took home a plate or a platter — trophies of the cause until, sooner or later, they broke.

The next residents were elected governors, first Patrick Henry and then Thomas Jefferson. Then the state government moved to Richmond in 1781; the empty Palace served as a hospital after the siege of Yorktown — and burned to the ground three days before Christmas.

Fortunately, Jefferson disliked Georgian architecture and had made elaborate sketches for remodeling, along with the floor plans and measurements of the rooms. These survived, ironically, to guide the restorers of what has been called America's most magnificent pre-Revolutionary building.

Now, almost year round, hundreds of

till found by accident. Touches of green, from melted salt, glaze six brick "arches" in the firebox; they supported a platform for firing pottery. Archeologist Norman Barka calls the early 18th-century kiln "the most complete found in North America."

visitors daily pay a special fee to walk through the reception halls and sitting rooms and ballroom, to admire the princely gardens and the handsome furnishings. Details of decoration change, with new research and with changing seasons, as at Christmas. I joined one of the groups to see the current display and hear the guide explain customs of the past.

In the dining room especially, I noted people admiring the shining glass and the table's four-tiered centerpiece, laden with fruits and sweet-meats. I thought of the difference between this display and the homes of the colonists themselves.

And as I looked around at the thoughtful expressions, at heads bent for a close look at details, I recalled Mr. Noël Hume's remarks about archeology and history and restorations. They reminded me of those I had heard from James Deetz at Plimoth.

"When we dig up broken pottery or slag iron or even a house foundation, I don't see them as mere fragments. I see the whole object that somebody used during a life in the past. It's an important part of our job to let others see this too—in the long run, nothing interests people more than people!"

After all, Mr. Noël Hume pointed out, the public contributes much to archeology, through funds for university departments and through admission fees at many historic places. The public, logically, should share the fun.

And by supporting research, as well as by coming in great numbers to see places like Williamsburg, Americans prove that they like to know about the people who built the country.

COTTON COULSON

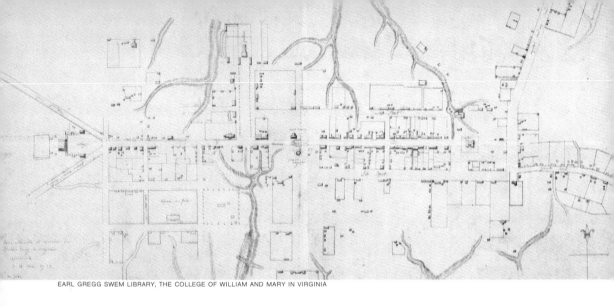

At Virginia's colonial capital, the Governor's Palace "has excited the public imagination as has no other Williamsburg project," says archeologist Ivor Noël Hume. An engraving from about 1740 gave details for the south façade. Facing a long green outlined by dots for trees, the mansion also appears at upper left on the "Frenchman's map," which came to light in 1909. Probably drawn by a French military cartographer to guide the billeting of troops, the map shows every house, tavern, church, and public building: an invaluable record for restoration since the 1920's. After the siege of Yorktown in 1781, fire destroyed the Palace; tiles, marble, and wood that fell into the cellars became clues to interior decoration. Today the Crown emblems of lion and unicorn recall the last royal governor, Lord Dunmore, who fled the town by night in June 1775.

*Resident of the Palace between 1778
and 1780, Governor Thomas Jefferson
sketched its floor plan and scribbled notes
of dimensions. His work gave restorers
their only drawing of the interior plan.*

*Today the elegant furnishings, based on
inventories of two royal governors, charm
thousands of visitors a year. Above, in
the dining room, a Georgian table stands
set for a dessert course. The reassembled
porcelain plate at left bears the arms of
Lord Dunmore. Its fragments came from
the yard near the kitchen; similar sherds,
apparently souvenirs of rebellion in 1775,
from various sites about the town.*

Before: 1965 — After: 1740. In a guest room of Wetherburn's Tavern, architects for Colonial Williamsburg stripped away layers of paint and plaster (below) to return fireplace, walls, and floor to original condition. Furnishings, from various locations, have survived two centuries. Below, roofers nail on shingles of the old shape but in fire-proof material. Gleaming candles now beckon visitors to an exhibit dining room.

149

A NEW NATION, A NEW FREEDOM:

I MADE MY FIRST unhurried visit to Yorktown as a boy of ten, and remembered it as a pleasant place with grassy ramparts, some tempting old cannon, and an enemy flag claiming a very small fort.

My father, who grew up in the Northwest, took the family to visit historical landmarks every summer—as a first-generation American, he may have felt a subconscious need to make our national heritage his own. Over the years we visited many historical sites; and when I became fascinated with the Civil War, he let me have a week's trip to the Virginia battlefields in return for my painting the house.

Tramping battlefields has been a sport of mine ever since. I go with friends: a garage mechanic, doctors and fellow teachers, a traveling salesman, a retired chemist, a used-car salesman, a corporation executive. Our ages range from 25 to 80. We all read military history and we all like to walk. We agree with the specialist who said his subject needs "not more documents but a pair of sturdy boots." We've toured the Normandy beaches, and the Western Front of World War I; the 18th-century fortress at Louisbourg, in Nova Scotia; innumerable Civil War fields.

We prefer to explore for ourselves. Year after year we've returned to the unspoiled Wilderness area in Virginia. There, once, I asked a park ranger about a segment of 1864 trench we couldn't find. I can still hear him drawling, "How would I know? There's not one fool in a hundred goes back in there!"

We've tramped around the Yorktown area several times, but always in search of Civil War earthworks built in 1862. We hunt these out on our own, in the woods, with old maps and reports in hand; for we've learned to enjoy the "skilled game" that the English historian G. M. Trevelyan called "almost the greatest of out-door intellectual pleasures." By comparison, well-marked remains from the Revolutionary War seem tame stuff indeed.

But in 1975 I decided to revisit Yorktown, and I arrived on the weekend of annual ceremonies commemorating the British surrender of October 19, 1781. Yorktown had its past on display for five thousand visitors. Ladies of the Yorktown Womens Club, in colonial dress, served biscuits and Brunswick stew in the gardens of Georgian houses. At the Monument to the Alliance and Victory, dignitaries placed a wreath; at the French cemetery, a similar ritual honored the Allied dead. And if the visiting kids wriggled a bit during the speeches, they squealed with delight when Gaskins Battalion fired its salutes—a realistic performance by artillery crews in 18th-century uniforms.

As soon as I could, I escaped the crowds—to see what the ground would tell me about the events that took place here. I spent the afternoon wandering over what is left of the British defenses. A kindred spirit, the journalist Benson Lossing, had come here in 1848 gathering data for his useful *Pictorial Field-Book of the Revolution.* He described the works then: 12 to 15 feet high, covered by "a hard sward." He thought they would stand half a century.

Lossing reckoned without the Confederate engineers who incorporated the British works into a new defense line in 1862 and altered them for greater protec-

YORKTOWN AND ANTIETAM

tion against powerful Union siege guns.

Actually the basic rules of fortification had not changed much from 1781. The town was surrounded by a wide mound of earth, the rampart. Its inner slope had ramps for easier movement of men and artillery. The outer slope was crowned by a parapet, usually about 18 feet thick and 6 feet high. This earth came from a ditch outside, itself an obstacle to attacking infantry. Sometimes the defenders built a wooden palisade in the ditch; and in the detached little forts known as redoubts, sharpened stakes called fraises projected outward from the parapets.

Standing on the parapet, and looking out over the lovely York River, I could appreciate the importance of Yorktown in 1862. Its batteries denied the use of the river to Union ships — and if Union forces could outflank the Confederate defense line here, they might threaten Richmond. But in 1781 Yorktown had no importance whatever, simply in itself.

Yorktown *became* important when General Lord Charles Cornwallis brought his army here, after a frustrating campaign in the South. He had orders from his exasperating superior, Sir Henry Clinton, to rendezvous with British ships and embark his men for New York.

It was New York, a truly strategic center, that George Washington hoped to capture, with the help of the French army under the Comte de Rochambeau. The Allies would attack when Vice Admiral de Grasse arrived with a French fleet.

But on August 14, Washington learned

Revisiting Battlefields That Determined the Course of Liberty

By JAY LUVAAS, *Ph.D.*
Department of History,
Allegheny College

CANNONBALLS FOR CIVIL WAR ORDNANCE, FROM THE BATTLEFIELD AT FREDERICKSBURG, VIRGINIA.

that the French fleet was heading for Chesapeake Bay; and there, on September 5, it fought three British squadrons. In part because of confusing signals, the British failed to coordinate their attack. The battle was a clumsy business, but it sent the British ships back to New York for repairs—and it doomed Cornwallis. Washington seized the opportunity. His army and Rochambeau's reached Williamsburg by late September.

I've been analyzing such campaigns for years now; and this one strikes me as a remarkable achievement. What impresses me most is the Allied cooperation at every level. Rochambeau, the professional soldier, bowing gracefully to the wishes of a far less experienced—and less successful—commander. De Grasse, under orders to leave by October 15, staying to keep his blockade when Washington appealed for help. The French officers advancing money from their own pockets for American troops whose pay was long in arrears.

By comparison, in the final analysis, tension and rivalry and quarrels among the British commanders made possible Washington's victory at Yorktown. To understand a single battle often calls for a review of a war as a whole.

Moreover, it consistently calls for a survey of the entire field; and I got up early the next morning to finish inspecting the British position at Yorktown.

I had an eyewitness plan of the siege, drawn up *à la hâte*—in haste—by French engineers, brothers named Louis-Alexandre and Charles-Louis Berthier. It shows clearly how a deep and swampy ravine protected Yorktown on the west. Beyond

stood a work called the Fusiliers' Redoubt, reconstructed during the 1930's. Here I was touched to find a marker: to the men of the Royal Welch Fusiliers "who unbroken held this redoubt against Great Odds ... This tablet and flagstaff are erected, with permission, by their comrades in the regiment. 1957."

1957! They still cared. Sentiment and a sense of the past belong not only to the victors.

I went on to review the defense lines that extended to the famous Redoubts Nine and Ten, and checked a list of the British guns: 14 batteries mounting 65 cannon, the largest with a range of more than 2,000 yards. With these, and some 6,500 men, Cornwallis hoped to hold the open ground south of town, the only terrain suitable for a regular siege.

Between them Washington and Rochambeau had about 16,000 men, half of them French. Only the French had experience of sieges—Savannah excepted, Yorktown is the only formal siege of the war in North America—and they explained the procedure to the Americans.

The Marquis de Vauban had developed a nearly foolproof method of bringing siege guns and assault troops close to the enemy. Working at night, men dug trenches for protection against artillery. This began at dusk on October 6, and an American chaplain wrote: "Providence seemed ... to have drawn the curtains of darkness around us ... until the time of our greatest danger had passed by." By dawn the earthworks were high enough for safety, and crews went on to complete the first line of works, the so-called First Parallel.

The plan drawn by the Berthiers shows exactly how the First Parallel ran, and how the artillery concentrated its fire on the British defense batteries. Once the British cannon were reduced, the Allies would move forward, digging zigzag trenches called saps, and then complete a Second Parallel. The cannon in this line would blast openings in the British earthworks.

All this was standard procedure, and so was Washington's order that all the siege works be leveled after his victory. Nothing of the original First Parallel survived. In fact the terrain was eventually taken over for what a lifelong friend of mine calls "cow-pasture pool"—for a golf course.

Checking the position, maps in hand, I found the works being reconstructed; and at the Grand French Battery I could hardly believe my eyes. Gun platforms, powder magazines, palisades—it lacked only the artillerymen in blue uniforms to come fully to life.

Only one thing jarred. Green grass held the earth in place. The original works were secured by layers of gabions, baskets of wood containing soil. These, with bundles of brush called fascines, were like modern sandbags.

"I wonder how they knew what this thing really looked like," I heard a photographer mumble as he stalked the mounds. I've read enough about sieges to have a good idea; and I've studied one of the best pieces of evidence that survives. This is a painting by Louis van Blarenberghe, based on sketches by L.-A. Berthier. Rochambeau had it done for his own home, to flank a portrait of Washington; he would want it correct—if perhaps too tidy.

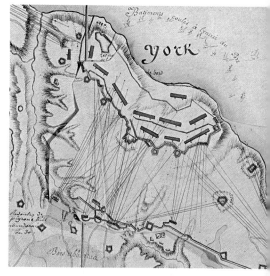

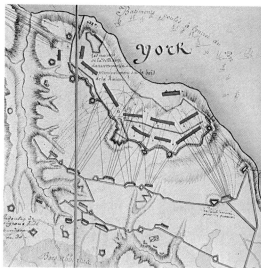

DETAILS FROM "PLAN FIGURÉ À VUE DU SIEGE D'YORK," 1781. BIBLIOTHÈQUE DU MINISTÈRE DE LA DÉFENSE, PARIS

I ran into a local resident, and asked if he remembered any signs of the original battery before the reconstruction.

"No sir!" he said emphatically. "It probably wasn't even here. Those fools have changed the site of the Surrender Field three times since I was a boy. Why, they even brought in truckloads of dirt for that battery. They sure did ruin a fine golf course," he added wistfully, "and now they want *my* farm."

I got a more technical report from Dr. Norman Barka and his colleagues, who began archeological research at Yorktown at the same time they were digging at Flowerdew Hundred. To me this was a real eye-opener. I had always associated archeology with Indians, old bricks, and broken vases; it had never occurred to me that I could also learn about earthworks destroyed long ago.

"Once soil is disturbed," Dr. Barka ex-plained, "it rarely resumes its original compactness. Soil stains always leave a distinct signature." Thus they had estab-lished the precise position of the battery.

Arthur (Barney) Barnes, who was su-pervising the reconstruction, told me how he knew that the works conformed to the rules of the day. "We could determine not only the width and depth of the ditch in 1781, but the edge of the parapet as well. Postmolds gave us the location of each log in the palisade, as well as the approximate size. 'Sleeper impressions' showed where the original gun platforms had been set on heavy timbers." Computing the cubic yard-age of earth from the ditch gave a probable height for the parapets: "About seven and a half feet." He grinned. "With exactly the profile recommended in the old manuals."

No historian could have proved that the French engineers had followed the rules, though one would expect them to. I was

gaining enough respect for archeology to learn without surprise that soil stains had even revealed the burst pattern of a large bomb—the kind of sight one witness had called "beautifully tremendous."

Barney explained how they had rebuilt the works, bringing in soil that would keep the proper shape, and why they had to use grass to simplify maintenance of the park. I left with an armful of plans that Dr. Barka had given me, and the feeling that I had reminded a fellow professor of an enthusiastic and unsophisticated freshman.

Returning to the siege works, I could imagine the frantic digging that completed the Second Parallel on the night of October 11—"the most important part of the siege," Baron von Steuben called it. The night of October 14 brought the most spectacular event: the storming of the two advance redoubts, Nine and Ten.

All day long the Allied siege guns had

Done "by the truth"—so Général le Comte de Rochambeau, in his own English, praised this painting of the siege, based on the Berthier maps and firsthand reports. The Americans have the sector nearest the river; the French infantry pass the now-quiet First Parallel, marching to the Second; Rochambeau, watching, flings out his arm to emphasize an order. Nearby, men prepare gabions, baskets used like sandbags. Terrain, fortifications, uniforms—all conform faithfully to well-documented details.

pounded them, "making holes sufficient to bury an ox in" as one of the American attackers noted later.

At dark the two assaulting columns, one French and one American, awaited the signal to attack. The Americans had bayonets ready, but on unloaded muskets. Success in such a venture depended on surprise and momentum—a man with a loaded gun would be tempted to stop and fire . . . and then, perhaps, to retreat.

Six shells fired in quick succession brought Lt. Col. Alexander Hamilton's men to their feet; and they quickly captured Redoubt Number Ten. The French at Nine were delayed by abatis—a primitive version of barbed wire, tangles of branches sharpened into spikes—but soon reached the top of the parapet. The British surrendered; and thereafter, the French colonel commented drolly, "We leaped with more tranquillity and less risk."

Those two small forts—restored in the 1930's by the National Park Service— were the key to the last British defenses. I went out to visit them before sunrise, to catch the mood of that attack; and I remembered the words of Lafayette: "You know, sir, that in this business of storming redoubts, with unloaded arms and fixed bayonets, the merit of the deed is in the soldiers who execute it."

That deed sealed the fate of Cornwallis. He wrote an explanation for Clinton: "My situation now becomes very critical. . . . Experience has shown that our fresh earthen works do not resist their powerful artillery, so that we shall soon be exposed to an assault in ruining works, in a bad position, and with weakened numbers."

On October 17, the British offered a parley; on October 19, the siege officially ended with the surrender of Cornwallis and his army. An officer of the New Jersey line recalled that the British officers were "like boys who had been whipped at school. Some bit their lips, some pouted, others cried." As for the Americans, one noted that they "could scarcely talk for laughing, and they could scarcely walk for jumping and dancing and singing as they went about." They had many dark days ahead, of sagging morale and no pay; but as it turned out, and as everyone knows, they—and the French—had won.

Save for its far-reaching consequences, the drama of the surrender and the storming of the redoubts, Yorktown lacks much of that human element that lends fascination to war. Despite its charm, the ground doesn't fit my notion of what Trevelyan meant by the joys of battlefield hunting. To him, "the charm of an historic battlefield is its fortuitous character. Chance selected this field out of so many, that low wall, this gentle slope of grass . . . a farm or straggling hedge, to turn the tide of war and decide the fate of nations and of creeds."

Chance played little role in an 18th-century siege, which was a matter of rules and routine. A siege was exacting, but not meant to be exciting.

Not so with a battle. Often, as Napoleon said, the issue depends on "a single instant, a single thought. The adversaries . . . mingle; they fight . . . the decisive moment appears; a psychological spark makes the decision; and a few reserve troops are enough to carry it out."

Such a battle was Antietam, in 1862, one of the most fortuitous—and important—of the Civil War. Chance selected one Maryland cornfield out of so many, a rail fence and a sunken road, a stone bridge, "to turn the tide of war" against Southern independence.

Why did the Confederate commander, Robert E. Lee, pit 40,000 men at most against a Union army he knew to be more than twice as large? Did he court disaster without enough men to exploit a victory? Or did he, as his admirers claim, know George B. McClellan was not a general to be feared? Historians will never agree.

Partisans—and nearly everyone who reads about the Civil War becomes a partisan—still argue over the reasons why McClellan failed to destroy Lee's entire army when he had the chance. Decisive moments slipped by; he had many reserve troops; he did not use them.

On September 9, Lee issued orders for a march into Pennsylvania. There he could feed his army at enemy expense, and forestall another Union thrust at Richmond. He sent three columns under T. J. (Stonewall) Jackson to capture Harpers Ferry while the rest headed north. By chance, a

(Continued on page 164)

Volunteers re-create a crack unit of the Continental Line, the First Maryland Regiment. Jeff Hobbs carries the special equipment of a sapper, assigned to hack away enemy abatis or palisades with ax or saw. In a night re-enactment, a platoon fires a musket volley while an artillery crew touches off a "galloper," or small fieldpiece.

Sunrise brightens a defender's view from the last-ditch British lines to the distant wall of their detached fort, Redoubt Nine. At left, restored in concrete, the redoubt's sharpened stakes (or fraise) slant upward, British style; the French preferred a downward slant, to deny a foothold to attackers. At far left, a gunner's view from inside the Grand French Battery in the First Parallel, which opened a steady bombardment on October 10 with ten cannon and six mortars.

*Ebb of a strong spring tide exposes a skeleton on the beach at Yorktown
—perhaps, says archeologist Norman Barka, from a British burial
ground of October 1781. Below, on the battlefield in 1974, Dr. Barka
visits a dig; he rests a hand on one mortar bomb as his colleague
Edward McManus brushes dirt from another, and James Smith leans
over to watch. The five bombs found here, in the trench fill of the Grand
French Battery, weighed about 150 pounds each—and turned out
to be live, powder and fuses intact. Above: a French 9-inch howitzer.*

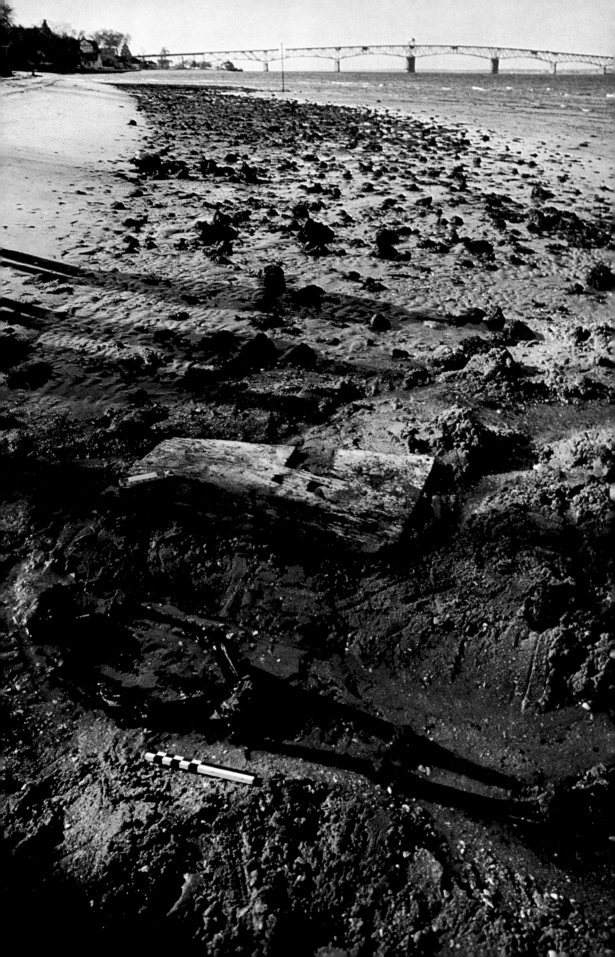

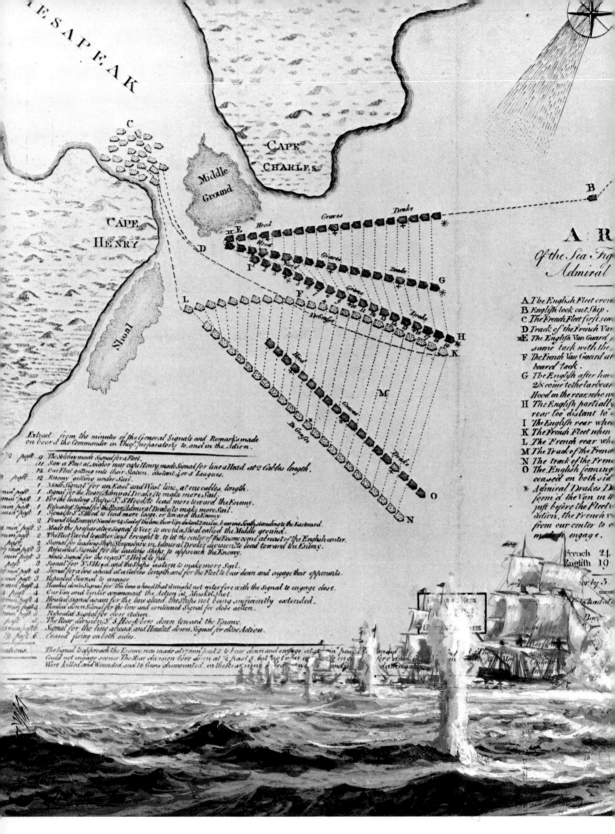

Signals of disaster: At 3:46 p.m. on September 5, H.M.S. London, *flagship of Rear Admiral Thomas Graves, R.N., flies contradictory signal pennants: red-and-white, ordering "all ships form line ahead," solid red for "engage the enemy." Unsure which to obey, Rear Admiral Sir*

DIAGRAM FROM "TWO LETTERS FROM W. GRAVES, ESQ....," PRIVATELY CIRCULATED IN LONDON IN 1782.

Samuel Hood did not open fire until 5:25 — too late. Count de Grasse and his French fleet remained in control of Chesapeake Bay, and of Cornwallis's fate. Background: a chart drawn in controversy over the Royal Navy's failure, which made Cornwallis's surrender inevitable.

One nation — or two? The Civil War must decide. In 1862, Robert E. Lee led a Confederate army into Maryland; George B. McClellan, the Union forces that met Lee in battle near Sharpsburg.

copy of his orders fell into the hands of a Union private, wrapped around a couple of cigars.

Reading those orders, McClellan saw his opportunity, as he put it, to "whip Bobbie Lee." But he moved too slowly. Lee had time to concentrate most of his men near the town of Sharpsburg, behind Antietam Creek. McClellan did not attack until September 17. And then his forces made three separate attacks — his right in the morning, his center about midday, his left in the afternoon. In each phase, the Rebels held, by the narrowest margin.

That outline is easy to understand, but Antietam is a deceptive battle. It has been thirty years since my first visit to the field, but I remember my initial impressions. Confusion! My father and I drove around the asphalt park roads and in an hour and a half we had seen the ground. I dutifully read every marker — I had just been devouring Douglas Southall Freeman's *Lee's Lieutenants*. But I was muddled.

Since then I've observed many other cars at Antietam, and I can see myself in most of them. Armed with a book or two and some maps, the driver cruises along from one marker to the next. He starts, perhaps, at Cornfield Avenue.

In this area, in early morning, McClellan threw Joseph Hooker's I Corps against Jackson's two divisions. Their men tangled head-on in a cornfield — *the* cornfield. Within minutes, General Hooker reported, "every stalk of corn in the ... greater part of the field was cut as closely as could have been done with a knife, and the slain lay in rows precisely as they had stood in their ranks. ..." Attack and counter-

attack swirled back and forth in this sector until about noon.

On Cornfield Avenue today, the signs strike from every direction: Hooker attacks ... Jackson counterattacks ... Hood comes up ... three brigades from D. H. Hill's command ... the VI Corps ... The *Sixth* Corps? I don't even remember reading about them!

Undaunted, the driver takes on the next cluster of markers. As I grow older, I'm more aware of others in the car: a wife, determined to be understanding, and a couple of squirmy kids. The only stop they want to make is a rest stop. The driver is not Lee — he surrenders and plans to come back some other day to get it all straight in his mind.

Even this once-over-lightly approach can help explain the battle. On maps the terrain seems flat; photographs can exaggerate a hill or flatten out a knoll. But the most casual visitor recognizes the undulating nature of the ground. A good driver hesitates to stop by a statue, because the narrow road dips into a ravine and a car coming up a little too fast might run into him. Just that sort of hesitation, that sort of blind collision, shaped much of the fighting on September 17.

Walking over the land makes this far more vivid. At the famous Bloody Lane, I overheard a comment by a young West Point graduate that says it all: "It's mind-boggling. It looks like open terrain — and you can't see a thing!"

And who has ever stood on Burnside's Bridge, key to the afternoon's fighting, and failed to imagine the feelings of men ordered to capture the heights beyond it?

Ripped by enemy fire, Union troops in a standard infantry formation drive for the West Wood—as drawn by eyewitness artist Edwin Forbes. Below, the Pry house, McClellan's headquarters, overlooks the fields where, on September 17, two armies fought to a standstill.

"A guy would have to be crazy to attempt a thing like that!" This came from a much-decorated major recently returned from Viet Nam.

It took a long time before I could appreciate how much there is to see at Antietam. When I acquired my own set of the *Official Records* of the War of the Rebellion, I found an entirely new war buried in those 128 massive volumes. They contain the correspondence and the after-action reports by nearly every commander, Union and Confederate, from the regimental level upward. With astonishing vividness, the *Official Records* have preserved the hopes, the thoughts, and the excuses that belong to every battle.

I've yet to find, for example, a subordinate who complained that he had more men than he needed. Or one who admitted that it was his regiment and not the Umpteenth Indiana next to it that gave way. There are gaps, many caused by bullets; there are contradictions; and there can be deliberate deception.

In his first report, McClellan said Maj. Gen. Ambrose E. Burnside got his order to carry the bridge at 10 a.m. He pointed to

165

the difficulties of Burnside's assignment and gave him credit for a useful attack.

Ten months later—after he and his successor Burnside had both been sacked by President Lincoln—McClellan presented an entirely different official version. Now Burnside got his order at 8 a.m. McClellan had sent an aide twice and then his Inspector General to prod Burnside into action. Without Burnside's unnecessary delays "our victory might...have been much more decisive."

I visit the battlefield each summer with a special class of career officers studying military history at West Point; and the first time I read these passages to the group, I heard someone mutter: "That adds cloud." He meant, I assume, that the inevitable fog of war is often deepened by the black cloud of distortion. A British officer put it nicely in 1905: "On the actual day of battle naked truths may be picked up for the asking: by the following morning they have already begun to get into their uniforms."

Usually the distortion is unintentional. Regimental commanders are first to write their reports; the brigade commander must wait for these to give his own account; and the higher up the chain of command, the later the reports are written. Stonewall Jackson did not prepare his report on Antietam until late April 1863; by then much of the information he needed had been lost, with the officers who knew it. Jackson himself was mortally wounded ten days later.

Luckily, the fine maps of the *Official Records* are usually accurate and detailed. Those for Antietam do not reveal much about troop movements; but maps surveyed by Lt. Col. E. B. Cope in the 1890's locate most units at different stages of the battle. Cope's information can be found on maps in James V. Murfin's *The Gleam of Bayonets,* a solid book on Antietam.

Yet, as Trevelyan said, working out positions on a battlefield is especially gratifying "if no one has ever done it properly before...." For years my friends and I shunned Antietam with all its markers, maps, statues, and tourists.

But when we did take on Antietam we found valuable links with the past. A number of farmhouses were significant in the fighting and useful reference points in the reports. Most of them still stand: the D. R. Miller house, the Roulette house. In 1975 Beth Roulette was one of the aides at the Park Service Visitors' Center, and willing to share a family legend. It says that her great-great-grandfather hid in his basement during the fight—"As kids we got a lot of ribbing about that."

Now, at every opportunity, we visit the scene and stroll over the ground. It has answered a number of questions. Take Brig. Gen. William H. French, U.S.A., whose division saw hard fighting near the Roulette house. How did it get separated from John Sedgwick's division when they had been side by side? No one knows for certain. Twice I've walked from the ford where French crossed Antietam Creek, following what seemed the most natural route. Both times I wound up where French did, before the Bloody Lane.

Even casual students of the Civil War have heard about the sunken road that became Bloody Lane, the center of Lee's position. The grisly photographs made there after the battle show Confederate dead stacked like cordwood. They give the impression that attacking the Rebels here was like shooting fish in a barrel.

But go out in front of the lane and climb the ridge where French's men shot it out with D. H. Hill's division for three hours. Even without the smoke of battle it's hard to see more than the head of someone standing in the sunken road. Look up at the high ground behind it. There were Confederate troops in a cornfield there, and artillery. Now you realize that it was the Federals who were the easy targets.

Here, once, I reminded a group of Army officers that several of French's regiments had never before seen battle. The 132nd Pennsylvania, "not yet organized a month," lost 396 out of 750 men and still, in its commander's words, "behaved like veterans and well-disciplined troops."

The officers fell silent, one muttering, "My God, look at the terrain they had to cover!" They knew from personal experience what it is like to lose men. One of them told me later, "Our formal training prepared us for everything except how to deal with losses." Probably not one had seen as many casualties during a year in Viet Nam as those who survived Bloody Lane saw in one battle.

It's easy to underestimate Civil War weapons. The musket of the Revolution barely covered 100 yards. The rifled musket of the 1860's had an effective range of at least 400 and killing power up to 1,000. The most effective infantry formation was the two-man line blazing away. There was

(Continued on page 176)

LIBRARY OF CONGRESS

UNSIGNED PENCIL DRAWING, PROBABLY BY ARTHUR LUMLEY;
LIBRARY OF CONGRESS

*Stubble in a snowy field — one of many on Antietam's
battleground — suggests the havoc in the most
famous of all: the thirty-acre field between the East
Wood and the West. In the morning, three vicious
attacks and counterattacks swirled back and forth
over the broken stalks, known as the Cornfield ever
since. The dead and wounded of that single field
numbered more than 12,000 within four hours.*

At point-blank range in standing corn, men of the Union's famous
Irish Brigade tangle with Rebels defending the center of Lee's line.
Today a rustic fence by a sunken road marks the Southern strong-
point that war renamed Bloody Lane. Here infantry and artillerists
held off Federal assaults for long, desperate hours. An observation
tower built in 1896 stands on high ground where Federal troops
gained a flanking position shortly after midday. From there they
concentrated a deadly enfilade—firing straight down the road. The
Confederates fell back in disorder, their dead covering the narrow lane.

Checked on an open knoll, T. F. Meagher's Irish Brigade reels under fire—from infantry in Bloody Lane and a cornfield behind it, from Capt. R. Boyce's battery on the ridge beyond.

"At this point," says Dr. Luvaas, "the terrain favored the Rebels." In the background: detail from an official map with Confederate commanders named in red, Federals in blue.

COTTON COULSON

On farmland made famous by battle, members of old Sharpsburg families
continue the chores of peace. Paul Spielman is a descendant of Joseph
Poffenburger, owner of land near the Cornfield; he now works the Mumma
farm that his father bought in 1924. Here he pauses by a rebuilt barn, where
Mrs. Spielman tends the Holstein cows. On September 17, 1862, all the Mumma
buildings burned except the spring house. Above, on a ridge near the National
Cemetery, a 12-pounder Napoleon marks the site of Rebel batteries: "a superb
artillery position," says the author. "From here, the Palmetto Artillery and a
Louisiana company with rifled guns were able to break up the Union advance
from Burnside's Bridge shortly after 2 p.m. That meant enough delay for
Burnside to fail—and for Lee to escape total defeat by the narrowest of margins."

Monument to failure: Burnside's Bridge spans Antietam Creek southeast of Sharpsburg. To cut off Lee's retreat to Virginia, McClellan ordered General Burnside to storm this bridge,

capture the ridge beyond (at left, above), and destroy the Rebel right. His attack, hard-fought but ill-directed, developed far too slowly — too late to assure a decisive Union victory.

*Headstones stand in silent ranks at Antietam
National Cemetery, links between a countryside at
peace and the violence that soaked it with the*

seldom much use of the bayonet, and men attacked with guns shouldered as on parade—an eyewitness sketch shows it well, portraying a charge by W. H. Irwin's Pennsylvania brigade near the Dunker church.

What it was like to make such a charge appears with painful honesty in the words of an infantryman from the 9th New York, a grunt from a bygone age. He fought under Burnside, on the steep ridges between Burnside's Bridge and the Hawkins Monument that now marks the high-water mark of that attack.

"Whether the regiment was thrown into disorder or not, I never knew. I only remember that as we rose and started all the fire . . . was loosed. . . . I see again, as I saw it then in a flash, a man just in front of me drop his musket and throw up his hands . . . . Many men fell going up the hill. . . ."

Stopping to assist a wounded officer, he was trapped in a hollow: "We lay there till dusk. . . . we had time to speculate on many things. . . . We heard all through the war that the army 'was eager to be led against the enemy.' It must have been so, for truthful correspondents said so, and editors confirmed it. But when you came to hunt for this particular itch, it was always the next regiment that had it. The truth is, when bullets are whacking against tree-trunks and solid shot are cracking skulls like egg-shells, the consuming passion in the breast of the average man is to get out of the way."

Yet men made these attacks, and men fought them off. And McClellan's unused reserves—as some of his officers saw—could have crushed Lee's army that day. They did not. Lee slipped off to Virginia.

Historians have argued the reasons why ever since. I've debated the point with my fellow trampers and with professional soldiers; and I have some conclusions to offer on the perennial riddle of which was the better army.

Man for man, even regiment against regiment, the two armies were nearly equal. Union equipment, of course, was superior. But Lee's was a better army—better organized, with subordinates who cooperated smoothly. All day at Antietam they shifted reinforcements to the most threatened spot. And the great difference, as every soldier knows, was leadership.

"To be perfect," says Trevelyan, the battlefield visitor must understand the men who fought there, "must know and feel what kind of men they were. . . ."

Yorktown and Antietam present interesting contrasts. Yorktown was decisive—but need not have been. Antietam was not decisive—but should have been. Chance played little part at Yorktown once the siege had begun; at Antietam, to borrow a phrase from Napoleon, the outcome hung "upon a spider's thread." The French and the Americans operated as one army; the corps and even the division commanders in the Union army operated independently of one another.

Yorktown was won cheaply as victories go—88 casualties among the Americans, 253 for the French, compared with 156 British soldiers killed, 326 wounded, 70 missing in action: a total of 893.

At Antietam, Sedgwick's division alone lost 2,210 men, almost three times as many as were killed or wounded on both sides in the siege of Yorktown. The

blood of more than 21,000 Americans. War records, official but incomplete, list the battle dead at 3,577, with 18,141 wounded. Although greater battles lay ahead, the toll of September 17, 1862, makes it the bloodiest single day of the war.

total: 12,410 Union and 10,700 Confederate casualties—dead, wounded, or missing—the highest of any single day's fight in the war and probably in our history. (When the Antietam National Cemetery was dedicated, on the fifth anniversary of the battle, McClellan was not invited.)

At Yorktown the works have been carefully reconstructed—indeed, this is probably the only place in the western world where the casual visitor can see what 18th-century siege lines actually looked like. The battlefield of Antietam is much as it was—one of the few major sites where one can get glimpses of the terrain as fighting men saw it.

Yorktown and Antietam do have one special point in common. Both decided the fate of nations. Yorktown tipped the scales of British opinion in favor of a negotiated peace with the United States. Antietam was not a victory for either side; but because it was not another Union defeat, Abraham Lincoln took the opportunity to issue the Emancipation Proclamation. The war for the Union became a war to end the evils of slavery; and it became impossible for France or Britain to recognize Confederate independence. If the Union stood to its purpose, it was certain to prevail.

Of visiting battlefields, said Trevelyan, "it is best of all when the battle decided something great that still has a claim on our gratitude." Yorktown led to national liberty, Antietam to liberty for all citizens. This is why these two battles reward our attention—they contain clues not only to our past, but more important still, to the American present.

COTTON COULSON

Between battles, Private Emory Eugene Kingin of the Fourth Michigan takes a soldier's pose: "Napoleon's gesture, hand in blouse," says the author. "Kingin's outfit was in the Fifth Corps, which McClellan never used at Antietam." Near Sharpsburg, on October 3, President Abraham Lincoln visits McClellan, whom he relieved of command in November. With Lee's invasion checked, Lincoln issued his Emancipation Proclamation and, in 1863, welcomed blacks to the military service of the United States — not just as state volunteers. Below, a guard detail of the 107th U.S. Colored Troops, who fought in the Carolinas in 1864 and 1865.

LIBRARY OF CONGRESS (ABOVE)

ALEX. GARDNER, PHOTOGRAPHER; LIBRARY OF CONGRESS

U. S. SIGNAL CORPS PHOTOGRAPH, NATIONAL ARCHIVES

FROM THE OBJECTS OF NOSTALGIA

ALL ONE SUMMER, as a boy of 12 in Colorado, a friend of mine hunted arrowheads. He never found any. But he did come upon something interesting one day: a scattering of shells behind a boulder —shells from a gun. He continued to examine the vicinity; and behind another large rock, at fairly close range, he found another batch of shells, equally time-worn.

A shoot-out. Red man and white man? Sheriff and outlaw? Cowman and sheepman? Good guy and bad guy? The evidence was unmistakable. The possibilities were obvious, the legends classic. But the true story was lost beyond recall.

At another time, in Texas, my friend explored the site of an abandoned frontier Army fort. No buildings remained, but the sandy soil yielded nails and other relics that few people bothered to pick up— then, at least. Today, he remarks, it would be easy to check these items with specialists and fill in a bit of local history. But the shoot-out site haunts the imagination, holds the authentic power of the past.

From the most rigorous erudition to the most lighthearted fun, the past has innumerable attractions. For example, a Maryland social organization that calls itself the Markland Medieval Mercenary Militia welcomes both "the serious student of Gothic languages" and "the casual member . . . who just likes to attend feasts." Any new member chooses a new name: Thorhall Halftroll, Twerp the Bandit, Morgan the Unbelievable, or Fred the Horrible. A would-be warrior can make himself a helmet from a propane-gas tank and go out to fire onions from catapults in an afternoon's mock war.

The authentic has its own special appeal. Civil War buffs take pains with tactics and equipment when they stage a re-enactment; re-created Revolutionary War units like the First Maryland pride themselves on valid drill and costume.

Authenticity and nostalgia meet in building up a collection, and today the range of "collectibles" is astonishing. It goes beyond artifacts and antiques in the classic sense. There's even a book, fully illustrated, for the single-minded Coke-bottle collector. All the Dixie Cup tops I used to lick and throw away as a girl— those portraits of movie stars and sports heroes are now in demand. I'm not sure anybody would want my schoolbooks if I'd saved them; but my comic books would be a prize.

Like other everyday items, they were clues to America's past in their own right. My comic books taught wartime patriotism, with superheroes using their superpowers to defend the U.S.A.; my schoolbooks eulogized that marble hero George Washington, who seemed stuffy by comparison. I understand him better now, by comparing him to Joe DiMaggio.

The Yankee Clipper stood on his dignity too, as his biographer Maury Allen makes clear. Teammates and fans didn't mind his aloofness—they saw him play. Well, Washington's public saw him in action, as politician, soldier, and President. I sometimes think my schoolbooks were too solemn for their own good; and I like the idea that people admired a hero of national beginnings, in an age of powder and ruffles, as they admired a hero of the national pastime in an age of shirtsleeves.

TO THE RIDDLES OF THE FUTURE

And I like the fact that at Meadowcroft the casual human record runs from today's thin-walled beer cans through colonial rum jars into the potsherds and stone tools of prehistory.

But in all this varied array, one set of items seems to me especially poignant: the glass arrowheads made by Ishi, remembered by a devoted friend as "the last wild Indian of North America."

He was born to mastery of the life of fishing and hunting and gathering; he learned it in the 1870's, in the Mount Lassen country of northern California, while his people dwindled to a handful and made what resistance they could to white invasion and massacre. They were the Yahi, or southern Yana. By about 1870 there were fewer than twelve survivors. Anthropologist A. L. Kroeber called them "the smallest free nation in the world." Like other California Indians they had made their edged weapons of obsidian; but when white settlement cut off the Yahi from their traditional supply, Ishi salvaged bottles from ranch dumps and cabin middens and worked them into serviceable arrowheads.

Finally, in 1911, the only survivor of his band, bereaved and nearly starving, Ishi chose to enter the world of the enemy. By good fortune he found friends among the scientists of the University of California, at Berkeley. He made a new life there with dignity, learning English and teaching Yahi. He enjoyed demonstrating his crafts, he loved to joke, and he endured tuberculosis without complaining until

A Heritage Reconsidered: Fun and Fables, Neglected Legends, and New Visions

By MARY ANN HARRELL
National Geographic Staff

NATIONAL PARK SERVICE

JOHN FULTON

JOHN FULTON

CANADA CENTRE INLAND WATERS, ENVIRONMENT CANADA

Digging into frontier days, excavators expose the frame of the steamboat Bertrand, *161 feet long. In 1865 she sank in the Missouri River, which later shifted course and left her landlocked within De Soto National Wildlife Refuge. She preserved a sample of 19th-century trade in more than two million items, from mining gear and farm tools to striped stockings and luxury goods like brandied peaches. At left, a detail from the side-scanning sonar record of an underwater survey by Canadian authorities in 1975 shows a 19th-century merchant schooner upright 300 feet down in Lake Ontario. Experts believe the ship to be the U.S.S.* Hamilton, *a vessel captured and armed to fight the British in the War of 1812. She and her sister ship* Scourge *went down in a violent squall on August 8, 1813. Archeologists working with the Royal Ontario Museum say the schooners survive "in almost perfect condition."*

Nostalgia, the zeal to collect, and the hope of a bargain bring customers to country auctions. At right, Vermonters surround an auctioneer (with cane) as he takes bids on a milking machine — still new enough for service, not yet old enough to catch a collector's eye. While nostalgia clings to the ideals of rural life in America, farmers have long made the most of innovations. Above, a late-19th-century steam tractor pulls a plow over grass-land; though efficient, such engines left operators grimy with smoke and dust. The new tractor at upper right has both air conditioning and a citizen's band radio. Says its owner: "I can wear my Sunday best in this cab, and I can be in touch with my wife."

COTTON COULSON

NATHAN BENN

he died in 1916. Ishi had moved from the hunter's world to a university museum — from the skills of Beringia and Jones-Miller and the figurine caves, to the skills of catching the right trolley car and paying fares. No life could illustrate more vividly the quickening rate of change that has marked human existence during the brief duration of the United States.

Change comes slowly in the archeological record. A spearpoint grows old-fashioned within a thousand years or so. Then change comes more quickly. Pottery alters perceptibly within a century. And now a year can see a subdivision spread across farmland or desert; a week or two can bring a skyscraper down.

Recently I rode into the District of Columbia with an archeologist I know. He was driving warily through a complicated interchange made trickier by detours for new cloverleafs and interchanges under construction. When we stopped to let a dump truck cross the lane, I asked, "Do you ever think what sort of ruin all this would make?" "Oh," he said cheerfully, "I see everything as a future ruin."

I could understand why he seemed to enjoy the mass-produced sort of souvenir so much: statuettes, ashtrays with state emblems, plastic models of national shrines, "gilded" plates with Presidential portraits in color.... Clearly he liked to think of his colleagues in the future trying to make a coherent picture from the remains of our civilization.

Robert Nathan turned the problem into a parable in his book *The Weans*. An expedition from Nairobi in the 79th century has achieved much success at the great sites of US, or WE. Findings indicate that its people must have been Weans. The name Washington has been read as Pound-Laundry, the probable capital. At n. Yok an enormous statue of a giantess, or goddess, has been found damaged, "one arm upraised in a threatening attitude." Her name was "Lib," or "Libby." She may have warned strangers that the Weans were an unwelcoming people.

Yet we have done our best for the future. The 1938 Westinghouse Time Capsule sealed up a selection of artifacts — can opener, telephone, doll, toy car, make-up kit, rhinestone clip, razors, swatches of fabric, sample metals — with a microfilm library. A 1965 version, expected to endure 5,000 years, added more than 20 million words on microfilm. It also held a Bible (Revised Standard Version), a bikini, graphite from the first atomic reactor, a 50-star flag, a Beatles record, an electric toothbrush. A seven-ton granite monument marks the place where the capsules await discovery, at the World's Fair grounds on Long Island.

We take unusual pains with our gifts to the future. Archeologists find trash heaps and grave goods, but nothing quite like time capsules. Our concern may stem from the experience that England's distinguished historian J. H. Plumb calls "the death of the past."

The past he defines as a living continuity. It includes the lessons and legends each generation would receive from its forebears. It adds value to the skills of survival, the arts of society, the sanctions of morality and government, the sense of destiny, the realm of the divine.

escape from everyday harassments and hazards. Bathrooms have hand grips for safety; public buildings and newer apartments offer ramps instead of stairs; to limit costs and chores, many "lawns" substitute green-painted pebbles for grass.

Today this past splinters and breaks up. Job skills cannot be learned at home. Manners change. Governments confront such possibilities as global famine. And for many, old faiths wane.

History, says Plumb, is unlike the past. "History, like science, is an intellectual process." It tries "to see things as they really were" on their own terms. It is detached, and critical; as disinterested as possible.

Jay Luvaas makes the same point: "A sense of the past is not the same thing as a sense of history." His examples are orations given at Yorktown to honor the victory of 1781. A French admiral in 1975 hailed Yorktown as a symbol of friendship between his country and ours. He did not, of course, call it a symbol of enmity between the France of Louis XVI and the Britain of George III. And the American orator of 1881 sailed gloriously over the issue: "Nor need we be too curious to inquire . . . into any special inducements" that led France "to intervene thus nobly in our behalf."

The past, says Plumb, has been a source of meaning, but not for everyone. "Nothing has been so corruptly used as concepts of the past." The historian's duty must be to serve mankind, "to reveal the complexities of human behaviour and the strangeness of events," including the shadows they have cast.

Plymouth, a byword of America's past, now includes a new dimension of her history. In a little-known episode after the Revolutionary War, the town rewarded a slave named Cato Howe for his service in the Continental Army. It gave him his freedom and 94 acres of land. Three other

COTTON COULSON

black veterans, Prince Williams, Quamany Quash, and Plato Turner won their freedom and joined Cato on the wooded site. Their community was called New Guinea.

My colleague Marie Bradby writes of it in 1976: "The day I visited New Guinea, a strong wind rustled the oak and pine trees. I was nervous — anxious to stand where my ancestors once lived. Just beyond the highway, cedar rails fence off several graves marked with simple fieldstones. A granite marker tells of the colony and the four original settlers who were buried at my feet.

"In a patch of sunlight about a hundred feet away, the partially excavated cellars of six small homes clustered in a small forest clearing. String grids crisscrossed the pits, marking the beginnings of an archeological dig.

"Dr. James Deetz, assistant director of Plimoth Plantation, led me along. 'Among the earlier communities of free blacks,' he began, 'this may be the first one looked at archeologically.' He stopped at a cellar and gazed down at the fine stonework. 'Thought it was a trash pit at first; turned out to be a cellar, possibly Cato Howe's. There may be all sorts of neat things in it. So far, we've dug up clay pipes, glass bottles, pottery, coins, window glass, and bull's eye glass.'

"Three big earthenware jars have been uncovered at the site. Dr. Deetz thinks they were made in the West Indies and used for shipping tamarinds; they may have found their way to New England with the human cargo of the slave trade.

"These artifacts draw a fragmented picture of the four settlers and their families. Dr. Deetz thinks the men might have been first-generation African-Americans, or even African born. Building their houses so close together is a 'very un-Yankee custom,' he points out, much more like an African village. 'After all, these guys had 94 acres and they all plopped down together. And their small houses didn't exactly conform to the Anglo-American building styles of the period.'

"New Guinea sits on the Plymouth town line at a fork in the road — a parting of the ways. At some time the townspeople began calling the place Parting Ways. But that was long after the black settlement had broken up and been forgotten.

"It was Marjorie Anderson, a longtime black resident and a political science graduate from Southeastern Massachusetts University, who heard about New Guinea and revived local awareness of the site. 'For most of my life here, I've tried to relate to Plymouth,' she said. 'I knew my people had done something, so I was very interested in this project. It's the first history in Plymouth that I could relate to.'

"As Chairperson of the Plymouth Bicentennial Advisory Committee on Black History and Culture, Inc., she kept the town from using the land as a new cemetery. In April 1975, Plymouth set aside 15 acres at Parting Ways as a historic site. Now Marjorie Anderson hopes that some of the homes can be restored and a museum or library built at the site — a new center of interest for the town and its many visitors."

Half a dozen similar projects, blending archeology and history, are establishing details of black contributions to the

Rodia, spent 33 years raising them and setting in thousands of pieces of broken pottery, glass, bottle caps, and seashells. "I wanted to do something for the United States . . . ," he once said. "I no have anybody help me out. I was a poor man." In 1954, at age 73, he abruptly abandoned the project and moved away.

building of America. Other minorities celebrate their roles with appropriate pride. Many elements of the New World story take on new interest in the Bicentennial year.

For example, Louisiana is sponsoring an edition in English of Le Page du Pratz' *Histoire de la Louisiane.* The introduction stresses his account of the Natchez war against the French—as an American revolt against European oppression. That the rebels were Indians, and unsuccessful, weighs less with the writer than their love of freedom.

None of my schoolbooks mentioned that incident, or the black soldiers of the Revolution, or Mistress Margaret Brent's request for the right to vote. Our past turns out to be an incomplete story.

Our history is richer by far—the brilliant fleet that de Soto saw in 1541 deserves its place upon the waters with the packets that Mark Twain described in *Life on the Mississippi.* Our heritage includes Cahokia as well as St. Louis, the hunters of the Hell Gap points as well as Buffalo Bill.

"The past which mankind needs is no longer a simple one," says Plumb. The Makah Tribal Council makes the same point, and makes it well: "It is time that peoples with different backgrounds and ideas should see into each others' lives. There is just one earth, and we are all on it together."

If the clues to human achievement in America are varied and complex, so much the better—we can enter the future, ruins and all, with something worthy of the poise of Ishi in his change of worlds.

COTTON COULSON

Construction demands demolition in New York City—typical of urban sites where tax laws and zoning regulations can make it more profitable to tear down an old building than to restore it. Although financial problems have recently slowed construction in Manhattan, the rapidity of change from old to new remains striking. At right, below, high-rise office structures flank a surviving brownstone house, the favorite style for a New York family of means in the late 19th century. Below, a subway train bears illegally spray-painted graffiti, reflecting an urge for self-expression as old as cave art.

COTTON COULSON

"Living archeology" at the University of Arizona sets students to analyzing garbage in Tucson. From untouched or half-eaten foods, they determined that in 1973 Tucson households threw away 9,500 tons of usable foodstuffs worth roughly ten million dollars. In contrast, workers at the Koster site in Illinois detect minimal waste about 6400 B.C.: nutshells, seeds, a few bones stripped of marrow.

LOWELL GEORGIA

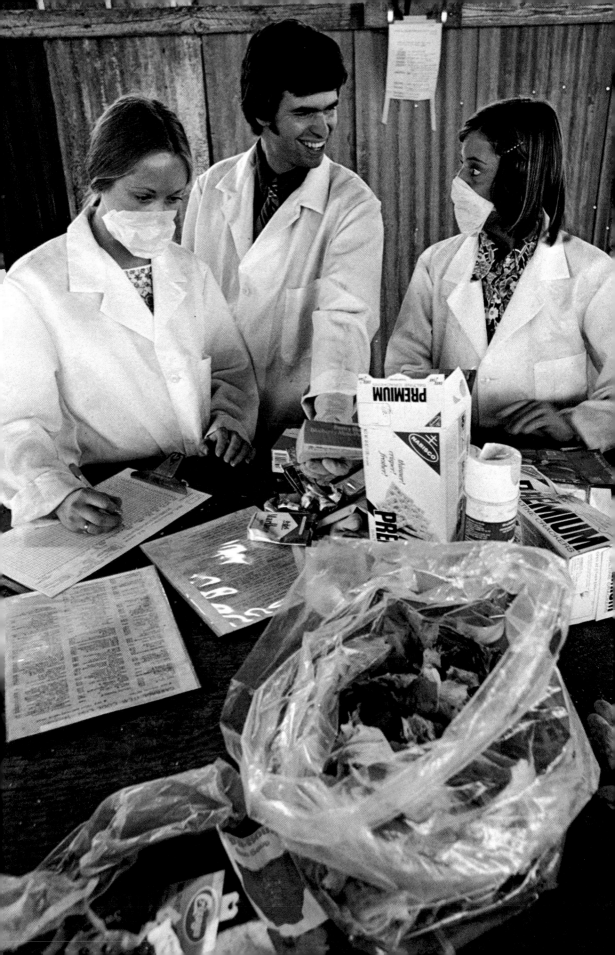

COTTON COULSON (ABOVE AND BELOW)

Cliff dwellings past and future stand less than 25 miles apart in the Arizona desert. At left, an ultra-modern prototype slowly takes shape on a mesa. Paolo Soleri, an ecology-conscious architect, designed it as part of a self-sufficient city to soar 25 stories when complete—after 10 to 20 years. Named Arcosanti, it will contain businesses, greenhouses for producing food and energy, and housing for 3,000 people. A skylight dome covers a two-story studio unit on the mesa (lower left). A ruin nearly 900 years old, called Montezuma's Castle, blends into the face of a cliff, protected from the weather. About 45 to 50 Indians, now known as Sinagua, chose to live in this five-story dwelling. To an unknown future they bequeathed a symbol of human adaptation to a harsh environment.

Index

Boldface indicates illustrations; *italic* refers to picture captions

Contributors

JEFFREY P. BRAIN received his B.A. from Harvard University, where he is now a Research Associate at the Peabody Museum; he earned his M.Phil. and Ph.D. at Yale. Self-described "half Yankee and half Southerner by birth," he focuses his research on the lower Mississippi Valley and has published technical papers on that work. Books in preparation include a survey of the prehistory of that region and reports on the Tunica Treasure, the Lake George site, the Winterville Mound site, and (with students) the archeology of the Natchez bluffs.

A New Yorker by birth, PETER COPELAND went to sea at age 16; he was a merchant seaman to age 28, and taught himself to draw between watches. During World War II he served in the South Pacific. He learned the illustrator's craft in the U. S. Army, served as a combat artist in Viet Nam, and worked for 15 years as a historical illustrator at the Smithsonian Institution. He has drawn for six historical coloring books for children, and recently prepared a book on working dress in colonial America.

LOUIS DE LA HABA—a journalist for twenty years and a staff writer and editor for NATIONAL GEOGRAPHIC during ten of them—became a free lance in 1973. His publications include articles on Belize, Guatemala, and Mexico. He is now a graduate student in anthropology at The George Washington University, specializing in New World archeology. A native of San Juan, Puerto Rico, he received his B.A. in philosophy from Amherst College in 1951.

A North Carolinian from Durham, MARY ANN HARRELL received her A.B. from Wellesley College, her M.A. from the University of North Carolina. Since joining the Society's staff in 1958, she has been a correspondence clerk, a researcher for NATIONAL GEOGRAPHIC, and researcher, writer, and editor for the Special Publications Division. She has written for *The White House: An Historic Guide* and *Equal Justice Under Law,* both produced by the Society as a public service.

A native of Kinston, North Carolina, TEE LOFTIN received her B.J. from the University of Missouri School of Journalism, her M.A. from American University in Washington, D. C. She worked on newspaper reporting, radio and television, and as a free lance before joining the Society's staff in 1967. Her contributions to Special Publications include a biography of Herman Hollerith for *Those Inventive Americans* (1971) as well as *The Wild Shores: America's Beginnings* (1974).

JAY LUVAAS earned his A.B. at Allegheny College, where he now teaches, his Ph.D. at Duke University. His publications include *The Military Legacy of the Civil War* and *The Education of an Army: British Military Thought 1815-1940.* He edited *Dear Miss Em: General Eichelberger's War in the Pacific, 1942-45.* Co-editor of the West Point Military Library, he served as the first visiting professor of military history at the U. S. Military Academy, 1972-1973. He is currently working on a study of the generalship of Frederick the Great and a book on the evolution of the art of war, 1861-1865.

Born in Pennsylvania, DOUGLAS W. SCHWARTZ received his A.B. from the University of Kentucky, his Ph.D. from Yale. In addition to his fieldwork in the Southwest, he has taken part in an anthropological study in Italy. In 1972 he was elected president of the Society for American Archeology. He is currently director of the School of American Research, in Santa Fe; vice-chairman of the Secretary of the Interior's advisory board on national parks, historical sites and monuments; a member of the Harvard University Overseers' visiting committee, Peabody Museum; and president of the Witter Bynner Poetry Foundation.

The Society's staff archeologist, GEORGE E. STUART earned his B.S. in geology at the University of South Carolina, his M.A. in anthropology at The George Washington University, and his Ph.D. in anthropology at the University of North Carolina-Chapel Hill. With his wife, Gene, he wrote the Special Publication *Discovering Man's Past in the Americas* (1969, 1973). His current projects include mapping the huge ancient Maya site of Cobá, on the Yucatán peninsula, in cooperation with Mexico's Instituto Nacionál de Antropología e Historia.

Self-taught artist LOUIS S. GLANZMAN has won awards for excellence from the Society of Illustrators, Art Directors Club, Inc., and Salmagundi Club, all of New York. He has illustrated more than a hundred children's classics as well as three earlier Special Publications: *The Vikings, The Incredible Incas and Their Timeless Land,* and *The Wild Shores: America's Beginnings.* A native of Baltimore, he now lives on Long Island and specializes in historical works.

Library of Congress CIP Data

National Geographic Society, Washington, D. C. Special Publications Division.
   Clues to America's past.

   Bibliography: p. 199.
   Includes index.
   1. United States—Antiquities. 2. Indians of North America—Antiquities. 3. Archaeology—Methodology. I. Title.
E159.5.N37 1976   973.1   76-688
ISBN 0-87044-192-2

Acknowledgments

The Special Publications Division is grateful to the individuals and organizations named or quoted in the text and to those cited here for their generous cooperation and assistance during the preparation of this book: The Bermuda Archives; The Bermuda Library; The Hispanic Society of America (Priscilla Muller); Library of Congress, Map and Rare Book Divisions; The Metropolitan Museum of Art (Judith McGee, Suzanne G. Valenstein); National Park Service (Dr. Tom Lyons, Harold L. Peterson, chief curator); Ohio Historical Society, Archives-Library Division; St. Mary's City Commission; Smithsonian Institution (Don Holst); U. S. Department of the Navy, Naval History Division; U. S. Military Academy; U. S. Naval Academy; Virginia Historical Society; Virginia State Library, Richmond; and James Anderson, William A. Baker, Dr. Elizabeth Benchley, Howard L. Blackmore, Eric de Jonge, Professor Charles H. Fairbanks, Alice W. Frothingham, Dr. P. E. Hare, Dr. Robert L. Humphrey, Jr., Albert Manucy, Diana McGeorge, Christopher A. Peal, Dr. Howard C. Rice, Bea Robertson, Dr. Peter Sly, Muriel Stefani.

In particular, the division extends its thanks to the organizations listed below for their courtesy in making artifacts available for illustration, and to the following photographers: N.G.S. Photographer Victor R. Boswell, Jr., p. 31 (bottom); David R. Bridge, N.G.S. Staff, p. 105; Cahokia Mounds Museum, East St. Louis, Ill., p. 70, bowls by N.G.S. Photographer Otis Imboden; Colonial Williamsburg Foundation, p. 123; Cotton Coulson, p. 41, p. 49, p. 71, p. 75, p. 151; Lowie Museum of Anthropology, University of California, Berkeley, p. 181; Mississippi Department of Archives and History, p. 89; Mound State Monument Museum, p. 91; David Grant Noble, p. 9, p. 19 (except center); The Peabody Museum of Archaeology and Ethnology, Harvard University, photographs by Hillel Burger, p. 19 (Mimbres bowl), p. 81; The Peabody Museum of Natural History, Yale University, photograph by N.G.S. Photographer Robert S. Oakes, pp. 96-97 (gorget); Smithsonian Institution, photograph by Cotton Coulson, p. 96 (lower); Southside Historical Sites, Inc., p. 139 (breastplate, halberd); Stovall Museum of Science and History, University of Oklahoma, photograph by N.G.S. Photographer Robert S. Oakes, p. 96 (upper); University Museum, University of Pennsylvania, Philadelphia, p. 31 (upper); Virginia Historic Landmarks Commission, p. 139 (helmet).

Additional Reading

The reader may want to check the *National Geographic Index* for related articles, and to refer to the following books:
Stephen Bonsal, *When the French Were Here;* Edward Bourne, *Narratives of the Career of Hernando de Soto;* William Bradford, *Of Plymouth Plantation,* ed. Samuel Eliot Morison; J. Burt and R. Ferguson, *Indians of the Southeast: Then and Now;* James Deetz, ed., *Man's Imprint from the Past;* Thomas Fleming, *Beat the Last Drum: the Siege of Yorktown, 1781;* Douglas Southall Freeman, *R. E. Lee* and *George Washington;* Garcilaso de la Vega, *The Florida of the Inca,* J. G. and J. J. Varner, translators and editors; Ernestine L. Greene, *In Search of Man;* Clarence Henry Haring, *The Spanish Empire in America;* Dwight B. Heath, ed., *A Journey of the Pilgrims at Plymouth: Mourt's Relation;* Sydney V. James, ed., *Three Visitors to Early Plymouth;* Jesse D. Jennings and Edward Norbeck, eds., *Prehistoric Man in the New World;* Henry P. Johnston, *The Yorktown Campaign and the Surrender of Cornwallis, 1781;* Alfred Vincent Kidder, *An Introduction to the Study of Southwestern Archeology;* Ruth Kirk with Richard D. Daugherty, *Hunters of the Whale;* Theodora Kroeber, *Ishi in Two Worlds;* Mark C. Leone, *Contemporary Archeology;* Joseph Plumb Martin, *Private Yankee Doodle,* ed. George Scheer; Charles R. McGimsey III, *Public Archeology;* Henry N. Michael and Elizabeth K. Ralph, *Dating Techniques for the Archeologist;* Robert S. Neitzel, *Archeology of the Fatherland Site;* Ivor Noël Hume, *Here Lies Virginia* and *Historical Archaeology;* J. H. Parry, *The Spanish Seaborne Empire;* Mendel Peterson, *The Funnel of Gold;* Howard C. Rice and Anne S. K. Brown, *The American Campaigns of Rochambeau's Army;* Jeremy A. Sabloff and Gordon R. Willey, *A History of American Archeology;* Robert Silverberg, *Mound Builders of Ancient America;* John R. Swanton, *Indian Tribes of the Lower Mississippi Valley...;* Sebastien Leprestre de Vauban, *A Manual of Siegecraft and Fortification,* George A. Rothrock, translator; Gordon R. Willey, *An Introduction to American Archeology;* Feenie Ziner, *The Pilgrims and Plymouth Colony.*

Composition for *Clues to America's Past* by National Geographic's Phototypographic Division, Carl M. Shrader, Chief; Lawrence F. Ludwig, Assistant Chief. Printed and bound by Kingsport Press, Kingsport, Tenn. Color separations by Beck Engraving Co., Philadelphia, Pa.; Colorgraphics, Inc., Beltsville, Md.; Graphic Color Plate, Inc., Stamford, Conn.; Progressive Color Corp., Rockville, Md.; J. Wm. Reed Co., Alexandria, Va.